ACCELERATED LEARNING

Increase Reading Speed With Accelerated
Learning Techniques

(Productivity and Use Your Acquired Skills to
Make a Passive Income!)

Velma Parker

Published by Zoe Lawson

Velma Parker

All Rights Reserved

Accelerated Learning: Increase Reading Speed With
Accelerated Learning Techniques (Productivity and Use Your
Acquired Skills to Make a Passive Income!)

ISBN 978-1-77485-278-1

Legal & Disclaimer

The information contained in this book is not designed to replace or take the place of any form of medicine or professional medical advice. The information in this book has been provided for educational and entertainment purposes only.

The information contained in this book has been compiled from sources deemed reliable, and it is accurate to the best of the Author's knowledge; however, the Author cannot guarantee its accuracy and validity and cannot be held liable for any errors or omissions. Changes are periodically made to this book. You must consult your doctor or get professional medical advice before using any of the suggested remedies, techniques, or information in this book.

Table of Contents

Introduction

The pace of life is speeding up. The quantity of information is increasing. The quantity of knowledge available is increasing.

School and work are becoming more in a race to the bottom. Many are looking for new than just ways to gain an advantage on the competition. How can you be noticed and shine in the conditions?

Society members are expected to learn more and more , and move faster and more quickly. Since the world is constantly changing, they must remain flexible to changing. There are many people juggling a variety of roles, tasks and identities. Many struggle to make ends meet.

What can we do to help people keep pace? Accelerated learning is a method. Technique and knowledge can be learned and taught at a faster rate.

Learning or teaching in a speedy manner will save time and cost. Training can be completed quicker. The process of obtaining qualifications is faster.

Accelerated learning is often viewed as more than just a practical option. It can be considered an alternative educational system that is in contrast to and even challenges the conventional notions as well as methods of study and teaching. As a type of alternative education, it could be seen as shaping the student in a different way, possibly by adjusting teachers and students to the current society. Perhaps it elevates students to new levels of understanding. It is regarded as a form of modern education.

Acceleratedlearning.info claims that accelerated learning is a professionally and scientifically developed approach to education developed over a long time. It's designed to create an environment that is more efficient for learning. Although it's conducted within a shorter time does not mean it's not as profound. Because it is more focused in its focus on a specific topic, it provides the opportunity for reflection and personal development.

Self-growth.com provides information on numerous ways to speed up learning generally, regardless of the purpose behind speedier learning and acquisition of skills.

After having defined the concept of accelerated learning (hereafter called "AL") This book explains this way of learning within the context of. Through a review of the fundamentals of the Western English-speaking educational universe We sketch out the way knowledge is conceptualized and arranged within the existing educational system. This way, the reader of this book can understand the basic pattern of thought that is the way in which ideas are organized in a way that the student or teacher is able to identify the most important elements in any knowledge body. There is a fundamental system for organizing thoughts. The more conscious regarding the structure and organization of ideas the better the learner and teacher can draw out concepts, principles as well as propositions and conclusions.

With that knowledge and knowledge, the student or teacher will be able to develop more effective learning strategies that allow for rapid comprehension and application of key concepts and jargon. This book is a focus on methods and collaboration. It offers tips for strategic speedy research, reading writing as well as listening and watching. It also provides suggestions for effective organization of instruction and study.

At the end the book benefits of AL are explained. Ideas on what and when AL can be used are offered, with reference to examples and instances.

AL can be useful for study as well as in work. Candidates can search for an AL programme of training or study. They could employ the methods that are based on AL.

However an individual student could develop their individual AL approach to a typical scenario of learning programmed whether at a classroom, or on the internet. It will be easier to organize a timetable of study, work as well as social or family life.

Education professionals can make AL programmes and curricula. AL can be provided by an school as an option. AL courses can be offered by institutions as an alternative. AL course is able to be incorporated in with shorter turnaround times at an institution that has different terms and options for its students.

A busy teacher can benefit from AL principles and techniques to devise and execute a efficient teaching assignments for a routine program. This is particularly useful when teaching multiple classes or multiple subjects in the same time.

There are numerous benefits of AL. In addition, there are numerous benefits. Learn more about this book to learn what you can about AL.

Chapter 1: Why You Should Improve Your Learning Skills

Why is it important to increase your knowledge? Let's talk about some reasons to consider improvement in your learning abilities an important goal:

Sharp Learning Skills Can Help you become productive, efficient and alert.

The ability to retain information and learn are beneficial to every aspect that you live in. In your professional or personal life, the advantages of these abilities are evident in every aspect that you live in. If you can learn quickly it is likely that you will spend less time learning new knowledge and new techniques whether it's related to your studies, your latest office venture, or your business.

Naturally, when you are able to learn things quickly, you will take shorter time to study every bit of information which means you will have more time for other things.

Additionally the ability to learn well can help to retain information faster and help you recall important information in a shorter amount of time. If you are able to recall information quickly that helps you to profit from opportunities as they arise. Because being a quick reader as well as a thinker, you are able to make fast, informed decisions.

If, for instance, someone asks your boss and a handful of your colleagues a crucial concern about the current project and you are the first to respond it is likely to make a lasting impression with your supervisor. Because of this the boss is more likely to choose you for the role of team leader or project manager.

Furthermore, having excellent learning abilities will help you learn new skills quickly and master them swiftly. If you're learning to make use of Photoshop or playing baseball, if your skills are well-organized, focused and attentive, you are bound to master both of them quickly and master them quick. Naturally, if you're proficient efficiently, then you're more likely to be efficient and increase your odds of meeting your objectives and getting the results you desire.

In conclusion Sharp thinking can help you master things faster, and help you achieve your goals and achieve them. If you want to be able to grasp things quickly and boost your productivity and become the boss of your own life it's time to focus on your thinking.

The next chapters will provide amazing strategies that, once implemented, will enhance your cognitive abilities.

How to Increase Your Efficiency

This chapter we're going to explore ways you can improve your ability to comprehend information quickly and master new skills quickly, so that you can increase your performance.

Think about the volume of information that you are exposed to or read each day. You read newspapers to catch up on current affairs and national/international news. You check your email for a variety of messages from subordinates, colleagues team members, as well as subscribed services.

You've read books, articles periodicals, proposal notecards from the child's teacher or school as well as a variety of other things that comprise your day. This indicates that reading is a talent you're most likely to utilize often and that will benefit you in all areas of your daily life. But, it is an ability that many do not value and will never develop.

When you consider the amount of time that reading takes up in your day-to-day life It is a talent which has the potential to assist you in improving your skills and one which you must improve since when you read quicker, you'll only need just a few minutes to read through the text you did not read for one hour. Naturally that when you read quickly, you can learn new quickly, which improves the speed at which you read.

The average person reads approximately 250 words per minute. If you had to go through a page with 500 words, it would take about two minutes. Imagine if you could multiply that rate by two and then go through the entire article in a matter of minutes or less, it could be a lot more enjoyable, wouldn't it? You could go through the entirety of a book, or a large article in half the amount of time, and then devote the remainder of the time to other activities or relieve stress.

Speed-reading can also help you grasp the overall structure and meaning of an argument, which allows you to understand the larger picture quickly and then make use of the information. Imagine, for instance, that your instructor is able to assign you a fifteen-page case study to complete in two hours, and then make a presentation about the subject in order to win a prize. If you're able to read quickly and quickly, you'll be able to read through the study study it quickly, and then prepare your argument with less time. This allows you to have more time to craft a winning and convincing argument will allow you to be the winner of the argument.

Now that you understand the benefits of speed-reading to enhance your learning capabilities Let us look at the most effective strategies to will help you reach this objective.

Chapter 2: The Mind-set You Need to Prepare For Change

"The primary step to take is prove it is feasible. then probability will arise," said Elon Musk and that is the same for those who learn to think quickly.

Before we get into the details of how to accelerate your reading and thinking processes, as well as your thought-processes it is essential to understand that with faster and more efficient learning comes discipline as well as emotional education. Because we'll be talking about methods that will benefit you over the long term making that change, it requires some effort. The first thing you must accomplish in order to begin getting better at thinking and learning:

Make sure you learn from mistakes. Life is a continual trial-and-error procedure. From the time you were born all the way until the time you die, you'll continuously making progress from the experiences you have had. While you grow older, you'll learn from your mistakes. Each when you make mistakes your brain's neurons create an outline of what did wrong to be able to refer back to it for future use. The brain cells are active every single time, so making mistakes can help in the brain's activity. If you are a person who is looking for intelligence You must realize that mistakes are an inevitable aspect of life and that reviewing your mistakes is as crucial as learning to gain information. Intelligent people objectively analyze their mistakes and is aware that the choice made in the moment isn't correct.

Consider your opinions in life. The greatest and smartest men in history have two things in common : they are all aware of the times they've been wrong and aren't willing to change their convictions. As you gain more information, you'll realize there are facts you learn may contradict your beliefs about factual facts. They'll cause you to reconsider your position while there are certain things that prompt you to say "this concept is better." You'll constantly changing your opinions on concepts in the course of time, and it is fine. Making your brain adjust to a variety of situations, particularly as you're learning, is crucial since it allows you to improve your skills over time.

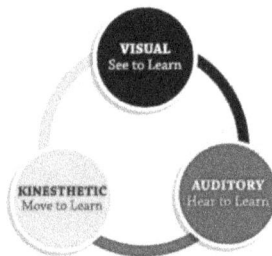

Raise important questions. While learning, it is necessary to revisit some of the beliefs you've thought as true. So, it's just equally important to inquire about the concepts you encounter rather than accept them without question. If, for instance, you come across a statement that is in opposition to your personal view Consider first whether that assertion is based on any evidence and if it's verified by others and, if it definitively is in opposition to your own beliefs about the subject.

These three elements are crucial in developing your thinking capabilities as well as in "warming your" your mind to the knowledge you'll develop as we advance. You can engage in the following activities to increase your thinking abilities in preparation for the future:

Find a topic you're interested in. It could be a current problem or an idea from a science-based perspective.

Note down your knowledge of the subject. Do you have any knowledge about this subject? What information about it could you impart?

Do some research on your subject, and note these aspects:

What you know already about the subject Things you learned about the subject that can support your notion

Things you learned about the subject, but don't support your notion

When you've written the statements, you should take note of way that the supporting and opposing statements differ from each other. Evaluate the credibility of each. Further research is recommended in the event that you need to.

Create a final description of your ideas about the topic you've chosen. Was it changed, or is it the same? Did you collect new information about it? What questions did your yourself to come to your conclusion?

Improved cognitive learning requires discipline This means that you'll have to repeat this exercise often over a period of time until you're able to effectively question the concepts you encounter, and also become more open to changing your ideas and being more aware. After gaining these skills, you're prepared to go on to more advanced learning and thinking strategies.

Chapter 3: Learning Effectively and efficiently

Humans are able to learn. can accomplish even without assistance from anyone else. The first experiences of a person's learning is through their own efforts. Of course, this is before he has even has a foot in an official school. This ability to learn on his own is complemented by the instruction provided by educational institutions. It is evident but this is that there's one thing institutions do not teach their students...how they can learn. To achieve meaningful knowledge and abilities they must be able to effectively and efficiently learn.

By focusing on the perspectives of people in the process of studying or studying to pass an exam, efficiency and effectiveness is the capacity to master all the information for the amount of time that is allocated. Learning is considered effective when all the necessary information and facts have been absorbed by the individual. It's effective when bits of knowledge are able to be remembered as required.

Certain people are more efficient and efficient when it comes to understanding or learning. Some individuals have declared themselves as average. The good thing lies in the fact that it is a trait which can be developed in the individual. There are some tips that can be followed by people looking to increase the speed as well as the quality of their education. These include:

1. Stop the practice of cramming: The practice of trying to study all evening or for a short time before an exam is often known as cramming. It is important to remember that forcing all the knowledge into the brain in this short time frame is not going to yield good results. The way to deal with this is to plan short, timed but evenly spaced studies. This way, both the capacity for memory in the short and long term of your brain may be enhanced.

2. Create the learning environment appropriately: It is about eliminating all things that can cause distracting factor

during your study. Distractions are the items that could reduce or completely impede your focus on studying materials. If your room is not noisy, has no TV, with adequate light and vents, and has access to all the learning resources should be sufficient.

3. The short breaks during the study sessions should be enjoyed. Brain, like we've mentioned previously, is an muscle. It gets tired, and as it gets tired the brain's ability to hold information decreases. Breaks of 5 to 10 minutes during the study session ought to be taken to enjoy. When you are taking these breaks exercising, walking or stopping for a moment to complete the work you're doing is a great thing to enjoy. It is best to avoid performing difficult or demanding tasks like washing dishes , or installing the PC because they could cause your progress in learning to a halt.

4. Highlight information when reading If reading is too much work you can try to highlight the most relevant pieces of information. Reading is the best method

to help the brain absorb information, doing it repeatedly could wear it out and cause poor memory storage. Mixing it up using the psychomotor movements of your hands will help ensure that your performance levels stay in the appropriate level.

5. Note important information by writing them down using flashcards, two objectives are accomplished. Learning is happening while writing and a revision material is what ends being created in the final. Writing can stimulate the brain to be more receptive to the knowledge it just acquired. There are times when the act of writing will produce greater outcomes. This is due to the fact that more senses are utilized to write.

6. After you have completed your study session. It is not recommended to engage in other activities, particularly ones which require your brain's cognitive capabilities. Relax your brain. The time between sleep and the study session is useful in developing memory over time and in the

retention of the facts that has just been taken in.

The ability to achieve high levels of efficiency and effectiveness during the learning process isn't at all difficult. It's just going to require determination and discipline for the student. After discipline has been discussed, the term "training" might be a thought. What is the best way to improve our brain's performance? Next chapter is going to offer answers to the question.

Chapter 4: Becoming A Learner

What are the steps to be a successful learner? You might think that you are done studying after you complete mandatory education, which most people do. However, this mindset causes people to be unhappy in their jobs just so they can make it through life, without taking in all the world offers. This isn't a great way to live. Life has more to offer that anyone could ever imagine and it is your mission to be as educated as you can during the time you've got on Earth. Albert Einstein once said "Once you stop learning, you start dying".

It's never more simple. You have the knowledge and experience of all humanity within your palm. The internet has changed the learning process. When you are stuck on a problem and are looking for answers, look up the internet. I'm 99% sure that someone else has had the same question as you have and has provided an answer. If you don't find an answer online? You can ask someone else whether they're an actual expert or an online expert They will be able to answer your question since they are what people love doing . The capacity and the desire to give information out and to do it in a manner that is openly and freely is what distinguishes the human from the beast.

There are many ways. In this day and age , there are more options to study than ever. However, there's a method of learning that stands out above the rest which is to learn through exploration. If you're exploring something, it's because you are enjoying it, or else you wouldn't bother to explore it at all in the first place. What happens when you're not able explore? Perhaps you prefer staying at home, or aren't in a position to get out and discover the world. It's okay, because there are plenty of ways to travel around the world. For instance, you can read books. It doesn't matter if it's non-fiction or fiction, you're exploring a world you like and are taking lessons from the experience.

There are numerous benefits when you become a perpetual learner. One of which is that you'll never get bored, or you are at least able to find it difficult to get bored. This is because when you are bored, there is something you can be learning.

You'll be a more content person. It's not easy to learn It can be difficult and you might want to quit. However, nothing is more satisfying than the feeling of satisfaction when you achieve your goals. The feeling that you get when you are creating a software program and having it come out without bugs or winning a tough match of tennis unimaginable. It's a good thing that things get better through time learning, and mastering a particular subject will help you understand the skills you need to succeed. Research has shown that the more determined we are, the more satisfied we feel. This is due because people who are ambitious always have something to be looking forward to and, regardless of what circumstance they're in they can see a bright hope at the end of the tunnel. You'll be a lot more humble.

When your purpose in life is learning then you'll be more appreciative of all that surrounds yourbecause you understand the steps to take. When you next meet someone, you should seek to gain knowledge from them, just as they are looking to get to know you better. Consider every interaction as an opportunity to learn regardless of their education level, background or previous experience. Because there's always something they are aware of that you do not. Your goal should be to find out that information and then apply it to yourself. I'm not advising you to be a sleuth around asking people to get information. However, ask questions and observe. By being humble, you'll be more likable and this will be evident your interactions with others. Instead of focusing on your own life, you should talk about them and their interest. Being so engaged in your friends will make you appear as a genuine and attractive person.

You can become a great teacher. One of the most rewarding actions you can take in life is to impart your knowledge to others which is how you're immortalized. In turn, the person you taught might go on to instruct others, and so on. Teaching is not just for students, but also teachers as well, since most of the time, you'll be asked questions that you've never considered before and discover you're learning something completely new while searching for the answer. You're a valuable part of the community. Being willing to study and are enthusiastic about it, indicates that you're valuable to everyone. As you grow older, the value will only increase. You'll be able to secure a lucrative job because you're eager to study. It's easier to find a beautiful spousebecause you're eager to take on the challenge of learning. If you're eager to learn, everything will be easy. That's why it's crucial to not give up in your pursuit of knowledge.

Kinesthetic and visual auditory

According to dictionary definitions, learning is the process of learning the knowledge or skill through experience, study or through being taught. However, learning is much more than the scope of this definition since different individuals learn in various ways. In terms of preferred ways of learning, students are categorized into three distinct categories, auditory, visual and Kinesthetic. This is known in the VAK theory of learning. It is vital to know that these categories define people's preferred methods of learning. Therefore, even those who are visual learners it is possible to be able to learn with an auditory method.

According to VAK theorists, individuals are able to identify a predominant method of learning that falls within one or the other in the VAK categories. However, the preferred method of learning could change based upon the topic they're trying master. For instance, when it comes to sports people may opt for the method of kinesthetic learning, which means that they would prefer to physically participate in the sport. However, the same person might prefer a visual approach to learning about programming software.

It is a VAK method of teaching is required of students all through school. From kindergarten to the third grade, you are taught kinesthetically, and from fourth grade onwards to eighth grade, you learn visually. Then you are taught in lectures. Usually , you're aware of your preferred method of learning at the point you're in highschool, but if you don't , I suggest you pay attentively to what you're naturally inclined to learn next time you're studying. Auditory learners are more likely to enjoy learning with audio. They might find that they speak to themselves frequently. If they want to read, they have trouble doing it in their head , and tend to read loudly. They would rather listen on audiobooks, even when they're able to read. If you're an auditory-learner, then you must devise strategies which rely heavily on audio. Group discussions and activities let participants to share their thoughts with group members. The act of reading aloud can be more effective than just reading your thoughts and it's beneficial to find an area where it is possible to read, without the other people around you. Consider putting your new content in an ebb and flow like poems or raps. While you're studying, you could be able to hear yourself singing. If you do, link the songs to the subject you're studying. The next time you hear the song the first thing that pops into your mind is what that you're studying, while listening to the song.

There are two channels for visual learning: linguistic as well as spatial. Visual learners who are linguistic prefer learning through written language, like writing and reading. They tend to keep the information written down even after having only read it only once. Spatial visual learners, however, struggle with writing and prefer learning materials by way of diagrams, videos, and demonstrations. They are typically creative and might find themselves drawing on paper in their boredom. If you're a visual student, you'll benefit from using images and drawing your notes with the help of diagrams or graphs. Visual learners are easily distracted, and it's best to avoid sitting near windows while studying and turn off your cell phone or any other device you are distracted by. If you're taking notes of the content It is important to emphasize important points using the highlighter or underlining. It is possible to be frustrated while in the lecture hall and listening to the monotonous voice of your lecturer even if that subject intriguing, you feel like you're falling into a deep sleep. If this occurs, and you're not keeping any details, it's an excellent idea to study the subject at your own time by using the mediums you are interested in. It could be in the form of an YouTube audio, video, or books.

Similar to the way there are two sub-channels to the visual, there's two sub-channels of kinesthetic education, there are the normal learners who prefer to learn through movement and physical tasks. Additionally, there are tactile kinesthetics learners who learn using the touch. Kinesthetic learners could find themselves distracted in the absence of activity or stimulation. When they read about a topic, they could find themselves looking through the pages to see what they can find to grasp the topic instead of taking time to look up the specifics. When they take notes, they typically employ colored highlighters as well as similar to visual learners they could be doodled frequently. If you're a kinesthetic student, it's essential to not get exhausted by frequent break. Engage in some exercise between classes to stimulate your body. You might find that the fidget toy like an squishy ball could aid you in staying focused and focused.

Chapter 5: What if You Like to be a Pro at it?

There's been a time. When you first start using an actual camera that isn't able to do every task for you the photos are out of focus or are underexposed. When you throw the ball, it wiggles and fails to hit your goal. You try the creation of a custard, but it curdles, then clumps. It's not enjoyable to make a mess of doing something. But do you know what? We are all. Everyone is. When you've not had the opportunity to learn a new ability, you're not equipped with that ability. It's a fact.

There is no way to be naturally proficient in anything. There are people with natural talent however that's not the case for everyone. Talent is a potentiality and skill is the ability. Talent may allow you to master a skill faster than other people, but you'll still need to put in the work necessary to develop the abilities. Jimi Hendrix wasn't born knowing how to play guitar, but he surely was born with a talent was later discovered. He learned to discern tunes on the spot using an ukulele that had only one string. He didn't learn to play on the guitar until 15 years old. Once the time came, he was able to make rapid progress and began playing blues at clubs with professional musicians of a different age within just a few years. The speed of his learning was naturally increased due to the talent he was blessed with, yet he was learning a lot. Skills to be acquired. The child had a fire which made learning the skills simpler, which allowed him to advance faster, but he needed to get down and perform the task. If he had not worked hard and honed his skills then he would never be able to progress from a simple strum on the ukulele's single string.

It's not every day that we get being born into a world with an innate aptitude, or a natural talent in any specific area. What's easy for one person may be an obstacle or even a challenge for someone else. It is crucial that we tackle our area of study, be it that is HTML fencing, coding mixing drinks or tightrope walking with the correct mindset, a strategy, and a few helpful tools for learning. If we can do this and we are able to do this, no task will be considered to be beyond our reach.

This book is intended to help you navigate your way towards learning skills and aid you in doing it more quickly and effectively than traditional methods. The life of today is extremely rapid, and for a lot individuals, there's simply no time to take on lengthy apprenticeships. If we follow logically through the steps in a well-planned sequence and focusing our learning on the utmost focus to accelerate our own personal development. This method of learning helps get on the same level with those gifted geniuses.

The following is an Accelerated Learning Bible? What is the reason for a Bible? Apart from its religious significance the term "bible" can be used to refer to any book considered to be a reference point in its field. We've tried that in this article. Like I'd like to suggest that if you master these techniques and apply them to your life, you could discover yourself converted.

It's not the kind of conversion that is religious however, it could be a change to an improved life that is self-directed, accelerated learning.

A Sense of Inspiration

We'll discuss the other topics in the future, but the base that everything else will be established is the right attitude. We must first be able to overcome the negativity that was evident in the first chapter of the book. Yes, it's hard to fail at something. We must be terrible at things before we can become proficient. Now that we've got that gone we can put it behind our heads. If you think failure is a sure thing, it's a part of failure. If you're unhappy prior to even starting do not bother.

To make the most of our skill acquisition process, we must build a positive mental attitude. This is essential. There are numerous actions you'll have to take in the direction of accelerated learning, but before taking that first step, you must to be confident in the course you're planning for yourself. Most likely, you've decided to study a subject you're interested in or you've decided, for whatever reason, you'd like learn, understand or even be able to master. Let's begin with that. If you're interested enough to be interested in learning it then you'll be able to build an inner confidence that you are in the same way you do. To help you succeed, I'd love you to take a few minutes to fill out a questionnaire. It can be considered homework if you're studying this text with specific aptitude in mind. We'll occasionally do theseshortlists, which are mostly introspective work throughout the the book. The forms I ask you to fill out are intended to help you clarify the path you want to take. I'd recommend putting them into an organized way in a binder in order to revisit them as you're required to remind you of your goals and goals. In the event that you don't already have a particular ability in mind when you purchased the publication, consider choosing one that you'd like to investigate. What has always been something you've wanted to learn to do? Use this book to give it a go?

Note your responses to the questions below on a piece of paper. These will help later. It is possible to label this as the your Primary Goal Inventory.

1.) What's your objective? What kind of knowledge or skills do you want to master? Give it a detailed description.

2.) Imagine yourself at your ideal level of mastery. What are you going to be able to accomplish that you aren't able to accomplish currently? Define this with precision.

3.) Make an affirmation in which you claim responsibility for the accomplishment of this goal. When you adopt the techniques that are suggested in this book you're committing to a system of self-guided , accelerated learning. Self-guided. You must be able to trust yourself in the achievement of your goals. Therefore, you must promise yourself that you will be a self-taught teacher who is responsible. Write it down. Don't be concerned about the grammar but just ensure that you're sincere. This is a note to you, therefore don't try to fake it. You'll be able to tell.

4.) A final affirmation this one that affirms that you are capable of doing it. It's important to believe in yourself. If you aren't sure if you believe it you can pretend to be this. You've been told to "fake it until you can achieve it" isn't it? It's never a bad idea to begin becoming accustomed to the idea of framing things in a positive way. You'll be amazed. Then, it becomes the case.

I understand the importance of believing in your self might be a bit more difficult to do than it is. There are many who spend countless hours and millions of dollars working on the exact same problem. We're going to take some time talking about this. It is important to remember is that your beliefs can be limited to the topic in question. Once you've mastered these methods of speedy learning, you will see an enhancement in your confidence level, which is the natural result of the success. However, for the moment, focus on the goal.

A clear focus is an important issue we'll continue to discuss but for now, all you need is to develop the belief that you will succeed in achieving exactly what you've decided to achieve at #1 on the goals inventory. If you're interested in learning conversational French then your goal is to expand your ability to converse in French. There is no need to believe you're meant to be a success. You don't need be convinced that the perfect person is available to help you. You don't need to be able to resolve any doubts that have made you anxious from the time you were a child. Simply believe that you are able to learn conversational French.

Take a deep breath

The subject of belief and trust is something worth contemplating on. In our case meditation does not have to be an Eastern one however I believe there's something to be learned from the traditions of these cultures. Do not be concerned if you've never practiced meditation before. This is a short mental workout. Find a quiet and peaceful location. Sit upright, let your spine support your body. Don't slump. Natural light is great. Natural sounds are great too. You can open the window. Close your eyes and relax your mind. Take a deep breath. Breathe in and exhale out. Naturally and slowly. Breathe through the nose, and exhale through your mouth. Do not rush, do not think or thinking about yourself.

Consider an instance of achievement or a time when you felt fulfilled. For instance, perhaps you took a walk for your college graduation ceremony. Do you remember how it felt when you received your diploma? Do you remember how it was a symbol of extra significance as a symbol of the effort you did for the course? The hours you spent studying? Do you remember the feeling it gave to step across the stage? And be greeted by applause? Take a few seconds. It doesn't have to be similar to the one you've seen. Find your own moment of joy. An experience where you were proud, confident and confident of yourself. If possible look for a symbol in the moment. The diploma. Applause. Applause you felt you were deserved! A thing that can be a substitute for your sense of achievement. It's a reminder of why you're working to do. For you, something that signifies success. The satisfaction and pride you feel after knowing that you've achieved something.

I've provided some examples, but ultimately, you have to come up with your personal. It should be personal. Pay attention to that moment the image or sound and then in your mind. It's something you'll be able to return to to boost your confidence when your confidence or momentum is slipping. It's called an emotional image, or a visual that helps you regain the sense of confidence and trust which we're trying to develop.

Preparing Your Work Environment

Another key element to developing the right mindset to learn is having the right environment. It's also individual. It's all about your personality and the things you're trying to master. One important thing to note is that stress can hinder our ability to learn. To let ourselves be open to the opportunity to take into account knowledge, we must to create a calm and conducive atmosphere.

The stress of anxiety can limit your ability to acquire abilities. Self-judgment hinders growth. There's nothing gained through pushing yourself too to hard. If you're an athlete you're likely to be familiar with "the zone." When you're in the zone it's not about trying to be as good as you could. It's about letting yourself relax to let your mind drift away from your own efforts. When you're in the zone, you're performing at your highest however, you're also kind of in autopilot mode. Your muscles are working and your subconscious. You're not focusing on your thoughts. Therefore, the aim is to create a space which will let you remove yourself from the midst of your own effort and to inspire you to keep in mind the goal you set out to achieve. Your workplace, if carefully planned, will naturally invoke your favorite image.

What are we planning to incorporate into your work space? Your research? It's"study" because that's the kind of thing you'll be doing in it. I'm going to offer some suggestions for things to think about when planning your space, but want to note that different methods are suitable for different individuals. The suggestions I'm offering are based on what has worked for me, and what research and personal experience have proved to be useful. However, please come up with your own method.

1.) Eliminate distractions from your workplace. If you don't use the internet to learn the skill you're trying to master you should eliminate the use of the internet. If you're not learning how to cook, don't make food that is easy to make. Keep only the books that you'll need to use for your studies or to practice. It is important to create a place where you are able to do the work you require free of distractions that are easily accessible. What we're talking about is the concept of selectivity, a crucial notion we'll be revisiting several times. Pick what you want to work in and eliminate the things you don't. Simple areas, free of clutter, are ideal for the majority of people.

2.) Atmospheric elements visually. Lighting is essential to certain people. The fluorescent lights don't inspire me. The sun's rays in the morning and in the afternoon works well for me when searching for motivation. There's something special about it. Because of practical reasons I usually work and study in the evening, and for working at night, I like ample and soft lighting. It's well-lit, which means I can clearly see my work with no distracting, yet without stark shadows. If you're having difficulty imagining the distinction between soft and hard lighting, think of the differences between an unveiled lamp as well as the Chinese lantern. The lamp that is not covered will send lots of light but leave you with harsh gradations of lighting and shadow. When using Chinese lanterns, you'll still get lots of light, but shadows are subtle and gentle. They are also more relaxing. It is possible that you feel differently however, I'm going to share some of my personal preferences and ideas that have been proven to work for different people generally. The soft light can be soothing, and peace, as we'll discover later, can stimulate the areas of our brains that create new memories and establish connections between different things.

3) Aural elements of the atmosphere. Certain people prefer silence during their work. Personally, if my work environment is too quiet I get agitated. I prefer a certain amount of background sound. Noise machines can be effective however I also enjoy music. When I'm in the classroom I like to listen to different kinds of music than I usually listen to. My tastes tend to lean toward rock and roll, however, when I'm focusing on accelerated learning, I tend music that is classical music or certain styles of jazz. In the first place, there are there are no lyrics. Language is distracting me when trying to concentrate.

Additionally, research points out: complex styles of music can stimulate various areas in the brain. When complex or classical instrumental jazz is played it stimulates my brain, without disorienting it. I feel more intelligent. Perhaps a trick however, it is a valuable one that can help keep me motivated. Take a look, and do some trial and error however, try to create the most pleasant environment for your the confines of your studies. If you'd rather be in a quiet space then go for it. One of the topics we'll discuss in the next chapter is the topic of various kinds of intelligence.

The basic idea is that brains of people are able to be smart in different ways. For those who have a musical aptitude the presence of the right music can trigger the brain. For others it's just music.

4.) Include some motivation. Place something in your work space to encourage you and remind you of the objective. It's going be largely dependent on individual preferences. Some people prefer to post slogans and quotes or pieces of wisdom. If you've got some deadlines - like that your trip to France with the intention to speak perfect French is scheduled on July 8th - an old-fashioned post-it note with July 8th inscribed on it could be a source of ideas, but I'd be wary of inflicting pressure by focusing on the date rather than the trip as something positive. I would prefer to use an image. If you've thought of an emotional symbol that is effective earlier think about an image that will serve as a reminder. If you were walking across the stage during graduation Perhaps you can place your cap on display in your study area, where you can see it while you work. If your aim is to learn French prior to the summer travels A postcard that shows an inspiring scene of Paris could be a good idea. Be special and personal memorable.

A well-organized, peaceful and positive workplace can make a huge difference in mentally preparing yourself for the task ahead. We'll return to this concept in Chapter 3 in which various preparation steps, like work space preparation is referred to in the context of "priming on the engine" as they assist in laying the foundation that makes learning possible.

After your space is set up, it's now time to begin to work on it. You can make adjustments according to your needs but don't make house cleaning or redecorating to justify it. It's way too easy. Choose a solution that is effective or something that's simple and inspirational and then put on your best and go working.

Chapter 6: Speed Reading

As students, consider the amount of books you read each day. You're reading textbooks and online research, or perhaps even proofreading and editing your personal essays. You're even reading today! Reading is a talent that we consider to be a given. But here's the challenge. Are you a great reader or are you a superb reader? Reading is a time-consuming activity that if you're able to get from good to outstanding and you can free up some time.

What is it that you need to do to become a good reader? First of all, a good reader is able to read faster than the average. Additionally, they are likely to be more effective in their reading. This chapter will examine how to make that transition.

The basics of Reading

Have you stopped to consider how your reading habits actually are? If you consider it reading is a difficult art. The typical reading speed is about 250 words per minute. This puts the average reading time between one and two minutes. Imagine being capable of reading 500 words in a minute. It would save lots of time for other things.

It's even better! Being a better reader means you'll be able to understand the text better than before. At the end of the day you'll be able read faster and more effectively.

A quick note: Speed reading isn't an ideal option. If you are reviewing an agreement or another important document be sure to slow down enough to can comprehend each and every particular.

Breaking Poor Reading Habits

We acquire poor reading habits while we are beginning to learn how to read. It's a problem that isn't addressed because no one ever tells us these behaviors aren't good enough, and they grow into adulthood with us. To be a better reader you must change these habits. These are the most commonly used:

Sub-Vocalization is the method of naming every word you can think of while the word is read. It is like hearing the word being spoken to you in your head. You can comprehend a word quicker that you could pronounce. You can turn off the voice in your head while you're reading. It's not easy, but getting rid of this habit can speed up your reading dramatically.

Word-by Word Reading: It's slow and if you are only focusing on specific words, you're not getting the whole idea behind the text. Begin by separating words into two words in blocks and gradually increase the number of words until you're reading between four and five words at each.

Poor Eye Movement The average reader reads every word of an article individually. But, the human eye can take in the words of four to five at the same time. Begin by easing your gaze when you read. This will enable you to read large blocks of words instead of the word one at a. As you get better your eye sight, it will begin racing across the screen in a blazing speed.

Regression: It's probably the most destructive behavior. However, it is not common for people to do this. Regression refers to the process of having to read over an entire sentence to ensure you comprehended it. This is a major cause of slowing reading speed. Being aware of the possibility of regression can be enough to stop it. Do not reread a sentence unless you are absolutely required to.

Inattention Deficit In the end, some people attempt to multi-task while they read. Contrary to popular opinion the human brain is incapable of multi-tasking. So, when you're reading, you must be focused on the words. Switch off the TV and start reading. Distractions in the background can cause you to lose your focus. The most frustrating thing is you may not be aware!

The Essentials for Speed Reading

In truth, breaking any of your poor reading habits can make a an enormous difference to your reading speed overall. Below are a few strategies that will help you speed up even more.

Practice: Read often to build up your. Most students don't face any issues with this. The problem is that they're overwhelmed with information to read in the amount of time allotted!

Start with the easy material Start with Easy Material: If you're first learning to read speed begin small and progress to more sophisticated texts.

Be honest: Some documents are intended for slow reading. Documents that are legal and correspondence must be read through in entirety.

Utilize an object: For instance, you can swiftly scroll an index card across the page in order to encourage speed reading. This makes it easier for your eyes to stay at with that index card.

Skimming provides you an idea of the way that text is laid out. The use of words that are Bold or Headings are two ways to recognize shifts from one subject to the next.

Speed reading is an ability which can be learned by anyone. The main thing to be considered in this section is breaking the bad habits of reading. The speed alone isn't enough, you also need to be a proficient reader. Do not compromise quality for speed.

When applied correctly when it is done correctly, speed reading can help you free up a lot of time to focus on other aspects of your studies.

Chapter 7: The Accelerated Learning Brain is Incredible

Before we dive into accelerated learning and methods for mastering it, it is essential to think about one of the greatest machine you have in your possession that is your brain. Accelerated learning relies on how your brain is able to store, process, and retrieves information.Knowing about the brain's functions will be able to assist you in the future.

This chapter focuses on the background behind the techniques for learning that we will explore later on in the book. It will not cover all that the brain can do however, the information contained here will aid you in understanding the logic behind the methods.

Let's start by doing something simple. Make a fist in each hand. Put them in place by knuckling your fingers (as as if you were doing the impression of a fist bump). The resulting shape is approximately what the brain is. Each fist represents one-half of your brain. The brain typically weighs 3 pounds. It's about 2.5% of bodyweight. Your brain is responsible for about 20 percent of the energy your body uses. When you look at the calories you consume 20 percent of it goes to the brain's normal activity. There are foods that are beneficial to our brains, however we'll get into more detail about these in a subsequent chapter.

The Three Brains

When you think of the brain as one organ, it actually has three components to it. The brain is described in the form of "the three-brain" by the neuroscientist Paul McLean. The various components of the brain have evolved in the course of time as humans evolved into what we are now. The brain's components are the stem and the limbic system and the Neocortex. Understanding the function of each component of the brain is distinctive and very interesting.

The Stem of Your Reptilian Brain is inside Your Brain Stem

The brain's part is located in the middle of the skull. The brain is similar to a variety of animals particularly reptiles. Since this part is shared by all species, we refer to it as the reptile brain. The brain's apex is crucial to your essential functions. It regulates your breathing and blood pressure, heart rate as well as other autonomic bodily functions. This is where your fight or flight response is located.

The fact that this area of the brain reacts to your body's signals is crucial in your capacity to learn. When you're afraid or else manage to trigger your fight or flight reaction and your ability to think is slowed by your reptile brain. A fight, or flight reaction triggers an adrenaline rush, and your body's focus is on survival. The capacity to think is completely shut down.

This shift may not seem to make sense, this was an important survival technique for humans of the past. If ancient people were out in the wilderness and were able to spot a predator that was dangerous in the area, they could have been more damaging in the event that they had been overanalyzing the situation. It's ideal that your mind direct your body to an opposite direction. Although we can call this reaction"fight or flight," it may be better to name the response freeze, flight or fight. This better describes the manner in which people respond to threats.

This approach worked for our ancestors from the past however, it's not serving modern people in the same way. For modern students You will react by frightening, freeze, or fight when faced with situations that aren't really all that dangerous. Stress, fear, anxiety or stress may kick this response into the highest gear. This can be the case during tests and is a major problem for a lot of students.

If this thought is blocking your path this moment but we'll discuss ways to combat the mind blank response you may encounter. Being in the best state to learn is one of the very first steps towards accelerated learning. The brain-wave state that allows you to have the most access to the regions of your brain which are concerned with higher-order thinking is crucial to achieving success in learning.

The Limbic System of Your Mammalian Brain is your Limbic System

Although the brain stem is shared by reptiles with the majority of reptiles The limbic system, however, is mostly shared with other mammals. The brain's limbic system is more intricate and is focused specifically on the immune system, as well as the hormone system. In this area of your brain, emotions, sexuality, feelings and mood are controlled in addition. The limbic system contains important components of your memory for the long term.

For accelerated learning specifically it is essential to learn about the amygdala, the thalamus and the the hippocampus. Your thalamus acts as it's a switchboard. Visual, tactile and auditory information flows to your thalamus. Following that, the information is absorbed into two distinct sections. The top of both paths connects to the cortices of the brain (visual cortex auditory cortex, visual cortex, and the somatosensory cortex). The neocortex contains these components however we'll get to this part of the brain in the next section.

On the other hand on the other path, sensory information is relayed through the brain's amygdala. Your amygdala controls your emotions. Inside, it evaluatesincoming informationand looks for emotional connections for you. The brain's axons will determine whether there is the freeze, flight or fight reaction. The change in the brain that occurs in response to the stimulus will be controlled by your amygdala. Stress, anxiety, fear or threat (which are recalled by an acronym such as FAST) trigger the amygdala to trigger freezing, fleeing and fight reaction.

As we've said previously it is not possible to learn when you are in the state of excitement. Thus, excitement and joy are the kind of feelings we wish to create when learning efficiently.

The final part of brain tissue is referred to as the hippocampus. The position of the hippocampus lies located below the thalamus, and in to the center of the brain. The three components that comprise the limbic systems comprise two distinct parts (one located in the left hemisphere and another located in the right hemisphere). The hippocampus plays a role in the processing of short-term memory making decisions about which memories should be transferred to the long-term center and transferring the memories to the sensory cortices to store them. Apart from storing memories the hippocampus is also involved in retrieving long-term information and storing memories.

The limbic system's ability to control emotions and long-term memory can mean various things to how we learn. If you're feeling emotions that are strong, you'll be more aware of what's taking place. They act like markers on a page or post-its which are attached to the memories. The events that were emotionally rich even years back will be remembered more than events that are more recent and mundane.

If you feel a positive emotion associated with a memory there's a greater chance of it being stored in a good way and you'll be capable of recalling it. Learning is the process of creating memories of knowledge and skills and therefore, we need to bring positive emotions into our learning to ensure academic achievement.

The Thinking Brain of Your Neocortex

This brain region is the one that is most human that is located in the cerebral cortex. There are a variety of systems in the neocortex responsible for language, reasoning critical thinking, as well as abstract thinking. There are lobes inside the neocortex which are focussed on seeing, speaking hearing, touching, and speaking.

The various components of the neocortex play a role in increasing your knowledge of academics. If you are familiar with the amygdala's two pathways for information and the cortices of the neocortex will make an amount of sense. The visual information collected by your eyes will travel into the cortex of vision. Finding it is as easy as placing your hands on the side of your head. Below your hand will be the visual cortex.

The auditory cortex of your brain is situated in both the sides of your brain near your ears. If you place your hands in a cup and put them over your ears, it will give you an idea of the location where this information is being sent.

Third and last cortex handles the sensations we experience including temperature, body positioning as well as texture and discomfort. The third cortex can be located by drawing lines across you head's top, from one ear to another.

The cortices in all of them process the information that they receive and transmit it to another cortex, which is the prefrontal cortex. The prefrontal cortex is where we store our working memory. After that, however the brain becomes more complicated. If a memory was created to last a long time, according to the brain, it will go to the brain's cortex to process it. Visual memories are stored within the visual cortex as well as auditory in the auditory and the somatosensory kinesthetic cortex. The information is divided between the different cortices. However, this is a huge benefit to our learning. If you acquire information using several senses, your memory will be deep-rooted in multiple areas that comprise your brain. The two senses that are that aren't being utilized right now are smell and taste however, they are likely to be little in common with learning than the other senses.

Brain Waves: Four Types of

The brain's nerves that allow you to not just read this book , but to consider it too are called neurons. Every person has the same number of neurons , which is about 100 billion when research suggests that the number could be higher than 86 billion.

The neurons communicate with one another through intricate networks and each neuron can connect to as many as 20000 neurons. The number of connections that are possible are truly incredible. According to Richard Thompson and Robert Ornstein in The Amazing Brain, "The amount of interconnections possible among these neurons is higher than the amount of atoms in our universe."

These neurons and their network of connections connect with one another via electrical signals. Each neuron is receiving and exchanging like electric currents. They are also known as brain waves due to their behavior like a cyclical wave.

Brain waves are measured with an electroencephalograph (EEG). The device makes use of electrodes to monitor how often the brain waves repeat. The measurement is called cycles per second, or Hertz (Hz). EEG studies have revealed that there exist four primary kinds of brainwaves: Alpha delta, beta theta. The brain waves are linked to the mental state people are in.

Alpha

The type of brain wave have a frequency ranging from 7-13 Hertz. These brain waves are typically related to being alert, awake and at peace. In the state of alpha, the brain operates in its most efficient way. In this state we are adept at making use of the brain's resources as well as paying attention to. The majority of those who find"the "zone" can be found in this type of state.

Students will realize that the Alpha state is the most effective option to learn in. This state will enable students be more focused on your study.

Beta

The brain waves (with an average frequency of 13-30 Hz) are among the most powerful waves. Beta state is the one that is where we spend the majority times in. This state permits us to shift our attention between one task to focus on something else. When it comes to the purposes of driving and parenting this state is perfect. It allows you to concentrate on a variety of things at the same time. Beta state isn't the most efficient for learning because of the continuous shifting of focus.

Delta

The brain waves (with frequencies between 0.1 to four milliseconds) are the most slow brain waves. It is common to be in the delta phase when you're sleeping. This is also when that your body's self-healing process at its most effectively.

Theta

This group of neuronal waves (with frequencies between 4-7 the Hz) is on the slow side however not as fast as delta. It is possible to enter the state of theta as you're preparing to go to sleep or are in meditation. The brain is processing and storing memories during this time. This is among the reasons that getting adequate sleep is crucial. Since this state lets you to keep information in your mind and learn as far as the alpha stage.

It should tell you everything you must learn regarding the mind. This will give you the foundation for understanding the reasons why the methods in the remainder of the book are so efficient. But this isn't the final chapter of your education more about your brain. In this book, there'll be some additional information on the brain that will assist you in understanding the brain's functions. If you've liked this novel quite much I'd suggest that you research books on the brain. One great suggestion for a book is Brain Rules by Dr. John Medina. However, there are plenty of other books to browse for.

Do not forget to take to take the "Test Youself" section at the conclusion of this chapter prior to moving to the next chapter. The test shouldn't take very long, but it can aid in ensuring that you're retaining the knowledge I'm discussing.

Take a test

1.) The three distinct parts of the triune mind are the brain stem, neocortex and

_____.

2.) If you experience a mental shift from your freeze or flight (or fight) response which part of your brain is at fault?

3.) Visual, kinesthetic as well as auditory memory are kept in similar areas in the brain. True or false?

4.) The most optimal condition to be in to learn is:) Alpha b) Alpha c)Delta d)Theta

Answer key:

1.) Limbic system

2.) The Amygdala

3.) False. Memories that are flagged to be stored for the long-term are stored in the same cortex which processed the information

4) Alpha state

Chapter 8: Learning Faster and Smarter

According to Warren Buffett once said, "The more you know and grow, the more you earn". The second richest man around believes that the best investment that you can make is yourself. Learn about the wisdom that others have worked to achieve their goals throughout their lives through their books. This drastically reduces the learning curve and could help you avoid a lifetime of trial and failure. If you're always learning, you're always getting better and enjoy more satisfaction over the vast majority of men living lives of desperation and silence.

The books are now more accessible more than they ever have been before! No matter if you're on New York City streets, in a bookshop or using your smartphone, you can have access to the world's most renowned source of wisdom. The most appealing aspect of investing in books is that it's an investment that is guaranteed to never decrease by value. It is cheap, and increases in its application over time. The most prosperous individuals around are constantly reading and making investments in their own minds and their own thoughts, then you should too. Books are like mentors; you can get a lot of value at a very low cost and can refer to their lessons over and time.

Many people, however, consider reading as a job. In reality 10% of people who purchase books are unable to finish one chapter! The contemporary education system has forced people's beliefs away from reading books. A majority of students' education begins and ends in the school. They have a variety of reasons the reason they do not study or invest money in their education. The excuses are based on the same argument: they don't have the time or are unable to appreciate the value of books. If you are one of the prolific readers, you might be dissatisfied by the length the time required you to read an entire book, or that sometimes you get distracted by what you read.

The good thing is that is that it's possible to change things. There are many ways to assist you in reading faster and more effectively, but they don't recognize what's important to read and what is true about speed reading. I'll give you a an easy-to-follow guideline for getting maximum value from the book as well as how to read faster without losing comprehension, and also how you can take notes effectively to enhance your knowledge of a topic. It's a straightforward 3-step method that can be implemented immediately and quickly.

Step 1. Power Reading

Traditional wisdom suggests that striving harder is the best path to success in business and in life. Let's put this notion on the line. Bill Gates's wealth is around $90 billion. this is higher than the sum of the assets of the top 40 percent of Americans approximately 130 million. Does this mean Bill Gates works 130 million times more over the standard low income American? Absolutely not!

What you put in does not equal your net worth, or else we'll all want to be construction workers. What can we learn from this situation? Working harder does not mean more output. What is the most important factor that determines the degree of success in your life is your attitude to work and the ability you have to think strategically. This principle is applicable to books too. The thing people must realize is that reading with intelligence is 100 times more valuable than reading regularly. Reading with power is the same as being able to read intelligently. I've broken down this concept into four easy steps:

* What should you read
• When should you read
How do you focus while reading
* How do you extract value

What to Read

There are numerous authors who claim to be knowledgeable on the subject matter, however they've never actively participated in events. There are two aspects to being able to determine if a book is worth your time and provides you with details that are up to current: 1. the author's credentials or experiences and secondly. the speed of the information.

It is important to be selective when you go through the material. When your advisor's financial adviser is still to develop an investment strategy for their own financial future, would you trust them to determine the future of your own? It is best to only seek advice of those who have achieved tangible outcomes in their lives or have an in-depth understanding of the subject due to real-world knowledge.

The third requirement is knowing the subject and whether its principals come with a expiration time. The expiration date varies for every book, therefore you must make use of common sense in the various kinds of. Some books have a long shelf life due to their underlying principles that are timeless , while others are like berries expire just after the book is published. Contrary to what many have said, you don't have to evaluate the book's appearance by its cover.

When to Read

The majority of us have at most a couple of hours during the day to ourselves. The average adult is spending nearly half an hour on Facebook every single day. It is always possible to find the time to study and invest in yourself. If you're not able to do that do that, you must change your priorities.

It is suggested that, when you are seated for a book, you are given at least one hour to concentrate on the content in the book without worrying about disrupting your timetable. This time period of discretion must not be set prior to an important project or it could cause you the reader to lose focus, as described in the next section. This advice was directly given from Bill Gates himself!

Books can be classified into three major categories: how-to, fiction classics, and how-to. The fiction genre is not included in this chapter because of their limited value and relevance. offer. How-to books are immediately applicable and should be read earlier in the day to reap the maximum advantages. Classics are books that offer an unconventional perspective that drastically reduces the learning curve. They are meant to be read on a regular basis.

If you divide books into three categories and you are able to see the areas where you are most focused and adjust them accordingly. If you'd like some guidelines to follow I would suggest you read the basics of typing in the morning, and then a classical book later into the night. While this might appear to be an excessive amount of time reading the book, it was designed for the aspiring learners. Feel free to modify this guideline to your particular situation, however, make sure it falls within the guidelines previously mentioned.

How to Focus While Reading

As an avid reader, you'll need to stay clear of distractions. The termites are like the distractions which eat away at the foundation of productivity. There are two factors that could affect your focus in the moment 1. past events and future expectations and 2. environmental factors. The focus on the past or future projects can greatly influence your ability to focus on the present. If it all is all that matters take a note of 1. the issue that you are experiencing what you were experiencing, 2. reasons why it's not as significant of a problem as you think, and 3. the possibility of a solution. Create a list that is small and allow five minutes to complete. This will help you place the past and the potential future back in their proper place and help you concentrate on the present.

The other issue you might be confronted with is the tendency to get distracted by the immediate environment instead of the book in the front of you. While this might be a small issue in terms of shifting attention but it gets worse over time. It is best to eliminate an animal while it's still tiny. The most simple solution to the problems is to use the restroom and find a comfy spot to relax prior to your reading time. Be aware that books can be a source of information and should not serve as a tool to exercise muscles. Darwinian muscles. Don't be afraid of creases on the corners of your book to make bookmarks if you find yourself absorbed by one and you find yourself chewing over the book (I myself have done this myself).).

How to extract Value

While reading in a book, it is important to picture you as a mining entrepreneur. It is true that 80percent of the pages in many books are not needed. The purpose of these pages is to convince the reader to believe something or help them gain a better understanding of an idea. While reading a book you should imagine yourself as a miner digging through the dirt to discover the gold. This is the principal ideas the author wants to communicate. This approach is usually best with bigger books. This is the most efficient method that I have learned from my own experience regarding the best way to go about accomplishing this:

Read the preview of book

This is intended to aid you in understanding the main aspects of the book so that you can know what are looking for.

Read the first and final chapter in the book.

This will provide you with an overview of the entire book and give you a clear understanding of what you are searching for.

Read the table of the contents

Once you have a good understanding of what gold is and what it looks like, you'll want to know where you can begin mining. Make sure you highlight only the chapters that you believe contain gold. Then, you can eliminate all other chapters that are not related to the goal.

*Read the chapters highlighted in the book

This is where you'll be using your pickaxe. It is important to take notes about the key parts that comprise this part.

This easy method that utilizes Pareto's Law has been used by a variety of highly successful people and allows you to read just 20 percent of a book, and still retain 80percent of the value! The greatest benefit of this technique is that it can be applied immediately and requires any practice to master. Utilizing the power of power reading, you will have the capability to read 10 times more effectively. This allows you to read the book and read the most important details quickly, while not focusing on the pages that fill in.

Step 2. Note-Taking

You must know how to record notes in the light of techniques for power reading to improve your understanding of the book you're reading. Note-taking is used for two reasons one is. to help you retain more information on a topic and 2. to understand what's crucial when you return to the book. There are numerous note-taking strategies available, but I'd like to establish some guidelines right from the beginning.

It's not a good idea to note notes in the absence of an actual book. Keep in mind that the primary purpose of a book is to inform or entertain and not to showcase or show off and display, so don't be afraid to note notes within the text. Making notes on an external device like paper or laptop can disrupt your stream of thought, and will ruin the primary goal of understanding the most important information when you reread an article. All you need to keep notes effectively is a pencil and a highlighter.

Highlight only what is relevant to the principal principles you have that you have previously learned through power reading. Annotations are intended to help you to become aware of the information you're studying and to expand the market of ideas in your head. An annotation can be used to add a note to the margin explaining your reasons for disagreeing with an issue even why you are in agreement and add more details. Be sure to use good handwriting when you write in the margins, to avoid interruption to the actual text. Limit notes to a maximum of two sentences so that you can maintain quality notes.

It is also important to remember that all information is not all created equal. Not all information is worthy of highlighting and taking notes often defeats the reason for doing it initially.

Step 3. Speed Reading

Let's make one thing crystal clear. Nobody can show anyone how to read more than 22,000 minutes of words (WMP) without a loss in understanding. It's not physically possible. Let's hold a short discussion to discuss the ways that reading works. Reading is made up of four distinct but interconnected factors: saccades, fixations and regressions, as well as subvocalization. A saccade is essentially the movement of your eyes through the pages. This is required since we can only read via our fovea the smallest area of our eyes due to the density of cons.

A fixation is the interval between saccades when your eye concentrates on a certain word to help you understand the meaning better. Studies show that the eye is focused on 85 percent of words that are content (big beautiful, interesting, intriguing) while 35% focus on words that function (for and, and or so, etc.). The fixations and saccades are how we read, sifting between left and right and taking occasionally pausing.

Regressions are parasites which eat away the time you have, and serve as speed limiters on your memory. You may have noticed while you read an article that you were required to go back to read the book you just finished reading. While the practice is mostly ineffective Regressions are performed to help you understand what you might have missed. They occur more frequently when you read large, complex books that demand more of your concentration.

The fourth and final factor that is involved in reading is subvocalization. It is not to be confused with schizophrenia, it is the quiet voice in your head which utters that you're reading loud. Although this can act as an additional speed limitation, you shouldn't try to completely eliminate subvocalization as numerous studies demonstrate that subvocalization is crucial to the comprehension of difficult texts.

However there are a lot of limitations in the ability of us to read faster than a certain number of WPM. The brain is obsessed with insignificant phrases, you continually regress and your memory is unable to not handle too many pages simultaneously It is impossible to read as fast as you are able to mentally speak.

But with a amount of practice the average adult can increase their reading speed to about 700 wpm. This method should be followed at the start of each reading session. It is important to consider this method as a daily ritual to start your day with reading. Like when you prepare yourself to be at your mental and physical top performance with your morning routine by using this method, you're preparing you to learn at the best speed that you can. This method takes just 10 minutes to carry out during the ritual that begins at the start of the reading session .

It is comprised of four steps:

Underline Tracing

Peripheral Indenting

Snapshots

Skimming

1. Make use of your notepad to draw under each line as quickly as you can in two minutes , while retaining your understanding of the words. This visual guide stops the occurrence of Regressions, decreases how often you do fixes and accelerates the speed of your sprints.

2. Make a three-word indentation within the first word and three words back from the word that you are focusing on during three minutes. This will allow you to make use of a small portion of your parafoveal zone which you can identify a sentence from. Then you will begin to go a bit further into the area from both sides when you are familiar with this technique.

3. Only take two to three evenly distributed fixes for each sentence for a period of two minutes. This step isn't required as it can be very stressful and demands more concentration effort.

4. Use the three steps previously mentioned in order to read fast to be able to comprehend in three minutes. This will push your brain's speed to the limit when you've completed this workout.

It's similar like watching the same YouTube video at 2x speed, then going back to the original speed. In the initial few instances you'll notice the effect will fade very quickly. Like when mastering any other skill, learning requires patience, practice and discipline to become routine.

This reading strategy of three steps is to be used in the order in which it was written in the chapter. You don't want to keep a note of what's not needed to be read and you do not want to be reading what you don't need to be aware of. You'll want to be able to comprehend and read the essential information and like to get it done quickly. This method is fast learning in its very best form and should be utilized every time you take a book.

Chapter 9: Photographic Memory

It is impossible to conclude the process of rapid learning without mentioning the significance in the photographic memory. Photographic memory is also referred to as an eidetic brain memory. It involves the ability to recall names pictures, images, numbers and words with great accuracy.

To improve your learning speed you need to improve your memory and be able to remember important information that is going through your brain. The concept behind the concept of a "Photographic" memory, is it's similar to the image you have stored in your memory. You can access images and other content in your storage.

You can also look at the image whenever you wish to, or zoom into it, or even share the content with others. Many of us possess a memory of photos that lets us see the things we've seen all over again.

However, we must increase the capability by being aware of the ability and further developing it. In the example above, one might remember a specific street that you've traveled to or area you've visited before when you are asked.

A camera memory can be an asset for anyone who is keen for speedy learning. When you are learning you'll need to recall many previous lessons, which can help you maintain an adherence to your learning.

With a photo memory you will be able to master how to perform something completely new by using information you have already learned. While you study you will also be able to grasp the aspects and concepts, the steps to take as well as colors, along with other aspects of learning faster.

Different brain regions develop at different stages and the adolescent age is an important stage in this change. At that point when we begin to build an impressive memory, but other factors can also affect the process.

A few of these are the development of your brain, genetics, and personal experiences. The things you do every day have an impact too.

This book will assist you to determine your photographic talents and help you harness them by showing you methods through that you can develop it completely.

Be more attentive

The best method to increase your memory of photographs is to be vigilant. Don't just glance at things. See them as they really are, and incorporate the images into your head. While eating lunch, refrain from eating the salad by yourself and also take note of the different colors of vegetables. Make sure to take in as much information as possible about your establishment and the surroundings.

When you make this choice, the memory will be a memory in your head and when asked what you consumed at lunch the next day, you'll be able to answer. Even if it's difficult to remember the specific title of your salad you'll still be able to use the word "Salad" since you're attentive at lunch.

Some successful people depend on their photographic memory to reproduce the same pattern that worked for their past experience or in a previous transaction. It is also an asset for your organization because you are an employee with photographic memory as everyone will depend on your unique and accelerated methods.

Note patterns

Another method of giving your photographic memory an increase is to study patterns. Systems are the basis for full structures, so that if you can identify the trend of a certain concept or skill, you'll begin to build memories in photography.

What is the best way to prepare the classic Watermelon Cocktail? You purchase the watermelon, extract the juice. You then get all the ingredients (based on your preferences) and then you prepare your drink.

It is no longer necessary to be able to recall all the steps. If you could make your initial patterns, you will be able to master the technique anywhere and at a speed that is incredibly fast.

The next time you're looking to create an alcoholic drink with watermelon, think of the glass, the watermelon and the next action will be in your mind.

For other jobs that have more complex designs, don't fret about what you can accomplish. Divide the process into groups, take photographs of each one and save the images in your memory.

Practice remembrance daily

In this book, we've stressed the importance of practicing as it is the foundation of speedy learning. As you continue to practice, the more proficient you will become. The same principle is applicable to developing memories of photography through the act of remembering.

As a child, someone offered you a present, you remember. You also made sure that the person who promised you a gift kept his/her promise or else you'd be crying and throw temper tantrums.

Nowthat you're mature, likely aren't able to remember the most important events that happen to you due to the fact that you don't take the initiative to develop your knowledge by remembrance.

If you wanted to learn how to build cars in factories, you would need to practice recall to complete the task faster than you anticipated. When you join a car, it's like repeating the same process over and over again with only minor changes.

If you are able to recall the process by yourself with just one car, you'll be an expert by the when you put together the next car. Memory is a great tool when you have an image memory, and there's the way to determine this from something you do every each day.

If you are in the cab to return home at night, and the driver makes the wrong route How do you determine that the route isn't the right one to follow? It's because you have a memory of photos (subconsciously created) of the way that leads to home.

Recalling the past, you need to improve your skills until you become very proficient. Because of the importance of memory for our entire conversation We will guide you through the most effective methods for recollecting

1. Be curious about the subject matter you are studying

If you don't have a keen interest in what you've learned and you don't care about even recollecting any of it. Everything you learn should be something that interests you, especially if it's something you're compelled to know.

Inspiring people can lead to higher levels of memory!

It is easy to recall the things that interest you. This is why, prior to settling for an ability that requires accelerated learning it is important to ensure that you will enjoy.

2.Link the information you've learned with the information you already have

What you're learning today is likely to be related to something you've been taught earlier in your life. By linking them, you'll be creating patterns within your head.

This technique allows you to keep a particular idea in mind when the idea of another comes into mind. For instance, if you are currently learning to play an instrument, but played an organ before connect both experiences with each other. It is important to know the basics of playing one of the instruments in order to learn how to play both. The universe has a link between what we learn and everything else we do Find it and make use of it to increase the level of memory you have to improve your memory for photography.

3. Utilize bedtime

The time at night before going to get to sleep is another time to recall your memories. However, you have to be in this manner in order to make it succeed.

If you are getting ready to go to bed, don't just immediately go to bed. Make an effort to remember everything you've learned during the day in great detail. When you do this, you're making an image of the day for your memory.

Sometimes , even while you sleep you'll find that you are able to dream about the thing you were thinking about because it's stored in your mind. Make bedtimes and nighttimes occasions to strengthen your memory abilities.

4.Remember small things, it can lead to bigger issues.

If you are trying to improve your memory abilities, start by focusing on the simpler things before progressing to the more complex things. Start with your food, clothes friends, birthdays, anniversaries, etc.

In today's world it's difficult to keep track of what we've learned. However, that's the purpose of accelerated learning about. It helps you reach the things that everyone else considers "Impossible" or "Difficult."

Begin today and remember your child's favorite friend's name. Remember what you had for breakfast in the morning and your boss's wedding venue and all other things that is important to you.

If you do this regularly and consistently, you'll also be able to keep in mind those important details that run across your job, abilities and even lessons.

5. Try to remember in a noisy setting

The majority of people find it easy to remember and recall everything as that the environment isn't too loud. But, this is only not the "Average" scale. It is important to go above that since it's easy to forget when everything is still.

But if you must remember a specific detail in order to accomplish speedier results and you're in a noisy area What do you plan to do? And, most importantly, if you are able to remember something you've experienced in a noisy setting this indicates that the concept that you've stored in your brain remains in your mind for the rest of time.

Therefore, start today practicing by consciously stepping out of your comfortable zone. When you're with your friends at a gathering be sure to check your thoughts and the concepts you've acquired.

The more you recall what you've stored in the back of your brain in unorthodox places and areas, the better you can strengthen your memory.

Make a memory castle

Do you recall what you had for lunch two days ago or even yesterday? You're now going through your brain trying to figure out what you remembered. This indicates that you've got some photographic memory abilities and if not have any, you're not the only one.

Many people don't remember their home phone numbers in addition to not checking smartphones. Many adults have difficulty trying to remember birthdays for more than 3 people in their family.

Many people are unable to remember more important details than the food they ate at lunch. You can remedy this issue and improve your memory by creating your memory palace.

If you've got an impressive memory and a memory palace, it is easy to remember your activities that you participated in earlier, and that includes the learning experiences you have had.

A memory palace can make things more enjoyable for you. it's like having an internal hard drive that in your head that you can access and download information. Let's say that you've created an app for a business and two companies are asking you to create exactly the same thing however within the same timeframe.

Instead of being overwhelmed by the job, all you need to do is return in your mind's palace. Find the information you require from the data that you've saved.

You'll be able finish both tasks with ease since you don't rely on manual direction any longer. You're relying on information that you've saved about how you developed the app in the past.

In the past How did people navigate around towns and cities without signs or Google maps? They utilized the same technique of building memory palaces. So how do you construct the memory palace? The first step is to establish a space within your head which is secure for the precise information you need to keep. The palace may be your office within your mind or even your house. You must contemplate the space more deeply as it is where you construct memories.

Then, you create the images of the things you need to keep in mind often. Look for objects that stand out with what you are doing as well as bright colors and even specific objects.

Your mind will step to your dream palace, and put the items you want to store there. It is important to do this by imagining yourself entering your memory palace and then storing the data.

Once you've finished take a break and get your attention for a bit. The reason you're in need of some distraction is to determine whether the data stored in your memory palace is still there.

Take a stroll and listen to music then go back to your memory home. Take a moment to reflect on the data you have stored and can you visualize it in your head?

Do you have a glimpse of the photo?

If yes do that, then you've successfully constructed memories palace. What you have to do now is to continuously upgrade your memory palace by adding more information and expand the range of your photography memory.

You can build multiple memories in your mind by incorporating different types of content. Your brain is capable of handling so many more things than you imagine therefore don't believe it's too much.

Visualize your learning

While you master the new skill through the speed of learning method, you can imagine the whole procedure. For instance, let's say you're trying to master how cook the best spaghetti in your town.

Then you're ready to cook the recipe. You research to help you visualize the entire process , from the moment you begin to prepare the ingredients, until the time you cook. Your brain must be fed with plenty of different colours as you cook.

Consider the bell peppers that you'll be using and what length the spaghetti will take, color of the sauce, and the sounds coming from the kitchen. When you arrive in the kitchen to begin cooking, you'll realize that it is easy to depend on the information you had in mind prior to.

When you're done cooking, you'll have saved all the details from the entire cooking process into your memory. When you next need to cook spaghetti, you won't have to read the recipe word-for-word for a long time. You'll have clear pictures of cooking the spaghetti.

When you visualize the process of learning and imagining the process of learning, you can boost the power of your photographic memory, absorbing particulars and getting acquainted with all aspects.

When you're required to complete the same task with a speedier pace it will be faster than the deadline since you've got a photo memory.

Photographic memory can also work well with other technical abilities when it comes to rapid learning. This is due to the fact that it allows you to repeat an activity multiple times and this is why people call you"Expert. "Expert."

All you needed to do was to visualize the process in your mind. Visualization is achieved by taking pictures using your eyes and then recording them in your brain. Have you ever enjoyed listening to classical music or attended the opera?

If you did been there, you would be amazed at the capability for the band to play in a well-organized manner without the need to read on any piece of paper at all times. They were able to imagine the entire show in their minds and create photographic memories.

Therefore, when it is showtime in various cities, they do exceptionally thanks to the ability to visualize. Similar principles apply to actresses and actors who are so adept in a particular role that they win an Oscar.

What did the actors do to be noticed? They employed the power of visualization using the use of a photographic memory.

When you next want to know something new, you should not mean that you learn by doing it passively! Learning passively is when you go through the material or perform actions while not paying attention and imagining the procedure.

Keep as much information about the technique and when you next need to perform the same task, you'll be amazed by the speed you can achieve. You'll have your mind readily available to pull out the photography sources you need to work faster and faster.

With a fully developed photo memory and other skillsthat you've designed, and you are now ready for the next chapter in our travels. The next chapter is focused on self-development!

Chapter 10: Directions Formulate Goals

Making goals is much easier said than done. What can I do to ensure that I've set a goal? What is the difference between a goal to an idea plan or a thought?

Pick a destination you'd like to reach by this program. Pick a simple goal with no intermediate objectives. Make sure that the goal matches each of these. If it doesn't match any of these make sure you correct the goal formulation.

What is the purpose of a goal?

The following structure may be used to represent a goal that is complete:

Initial state (current state) Then, Measures (path) and finally condition (target state)

In addition, a goal has a set date by which the goal is achieved.

Set goals for yourself regularly. You are only able to determine your actions to reach your goals. It is impossible to control goals that are dependent on other individuals and their decisions.

Example: I would like to complete this course.

Contraexample: My colleague needs trying to communicate more clear.

The point of departure

The basic feature of the situation is the rejection of the present the situation, or a flaw or defect which needs to be corrected. Take a look at your current situation. Consider what you would like to change or enhance. What is it that you dislike, and what frustrates you? A rejection of the given is typically an idea of what you would like to achieve. Imagine , if you were to reject and what this particular deficiency or defect is made up of. If all is the same, then goals are useless. Only those situations that demand the need for change will need goals. Goals are always linked to an alteration in the initial scenario.

Rejection of the given absence or weakness I can understand this very broadly, i.e., to be motivated by a positive goal for example, having a home that one owns, to make more money, etc. This could be described as being a "lack or lack of." There's an "gap" to fill or a desire that needs to be fulfilled, or the underlying problem that has to be fixed. The more clear you are about what you will not accept and what you are able to say, the more precise you can envision the you would like to see in the future.

Example: I make 300 EUR too much.

Contraexample: I don't like my job.

In this instance it is evident what the actual "shortage" is: I earn too little. Based on this information, a specific goal is possible to draw. The opposite example is too general to define an objective. It is only clear that something needs to be changed however, it is not clear what exactly.

The most important questions to ask are what causes your discontent? Do I make less than I should? Do I work for too long (60 hour work week) or at the wrong hour (shift shift work)? Does the work itself not a problem (would I rather be involved with people)?

It's definitely not the best solution to be blindfolded to make a change in your profession only to later discover that one of them does not like. If you aren't sure the exact reason you're refusing then you should consider asking yourself questions (what you are refusing, why and why, what do you think ... etc.).

The final scenario is the goal

When you are aware of the things that you dislike You then formulate the entire issue positively. When you are formulating a goal it is crucial to define precisely what you intend to accomplish. Make sure your destination is:

Realistic. It should define something is achievable - something that's within your real possibilities. The goal shouldn't be too tiny that it's insignificant.

Is concrete. The formula should answer the question: How is the first thing someone else can see that indicates I've reached my desired state? Also how do I know that I have achieved my objective?

It is formulated positively. Be sure to avoid negation. Do not formulate what you don't wish to say - instead, write the things you would like to achieve. It's impossible to perform "nothing," and you are not imagining "doing nothing" Our brains know there are no negatives. You can test this by not picturing penguins within the Arctic.

Example: I'd like to expand my knowledge in a class that is held during the evening.

Counterexample: I don't wish to stumble in the course of an oral exam.

The writing is fixed. Make sure to complete your formula with images or mind maps, diagrams or something similar. If you have a written description of your goals it is possible to exclude the possibility the possibility that you "forget" the goal you set or your objective changes as time passes.

If you're trying to be sure that your goal-setting formulation is clear enough, present your friend the goal you have formulated. Request him to write down what is his view of how someone might or may be able to achieve your goal that you've formulated when he describes the goal you're trying to reach Great. If he explains something completely and different, you could conclude that your goal-setting formula isn't clear enough. Ask yourself the W-question What do I intend to accomplish in what place and at what time?

Activities

Once you have a clear picture of the place you are and where you would like to go, you'll be able to determine the best way to reach your desired goal. What steps do you have to consider? Remember that, in the end there are endless options to go from A B. Make sure to consider alternative options when selecting the right approach.

As an example, think about an excursion for example, from Munich for example, or from the city of Munich Rome. There are a variety of ways to get to your destination You could travel by bus, car or train, purchase tickets for a plane, walk , take a mountain bike ride, and so on.. Each of these options work for the location you want to be reached. It is your choice to choose the one you prefer to use the most. Additionally, you've thought about what you might do if one of these strategies proves to be inappropriate for "walking."

Think outside the box - ask others for ideas on how to get from point A to B. You will be amazed at the number of alternatives you have to get to your destination, and also be aware of the byways and parallel roads. The most efficient method is not necessarily the most efficient. Sometimes, more important than the route. It is that it gives you pleasure - you are engaged - your curiosity or research sense is awakened.

Meeting

The final step is to set an appointment. What time do you intend to arrive at your goal? The goal shouldn't become an "endless project." Make a timetable for when you've achieved your goal. Take into consideration your resources - the time frame must be realistic. It is sensible to prepare the possibility of the unexpected and a place in which "something could happen in between." However, the duration must not be long enough that you "push the goal" and then lose interest in it. It could also serve as a basis to determine the actions you perform. Detours, even though in theory they accomplish the same end - could cause you to leave the field since they are time-consuming.

Chapter 11: Reading And Languages

Enhancing Your Reading Speed

Do you remember looking through an enormous book when you were in school, and wanted that you could just glance through the pages, and read as fast as you could complete the text before? Being ahead with your education is something you want to achieve when you're a busy student do you not? I'm sure I've experienced that feeling.

The best solution to this would be to study the art of speed reading. Speed reading is basically about doing as fast as you are able to. There are many people who struggle with reading speed and often don't realize the words they read as they attempt. We'll take an examination of what kind of techniques and tips can be used to speed your speed of reading up and get through those books that have gathered the dust in your bookshelf.

Have you ever noticed when you write or read you can hear yourself repeating the words that you are thinking of? That's called subvocalization. It is a human trait and lots of people use it. It has been proven to reduce your reading speed due the fact that you're pronouncing the words you are imagining in your head. If you can figure out an effective method to stop the subvocalization, you'll be capable of reading much faster than before.

But how do stop it? If it's part of human behavior and it's an established habit then how do you stop? It was my thought that similar thing when I first started. I believed that everybody else was doing it , and I had no alternative. But, there are some ways to break the habit. You can simply take a look at the words and make them register. Here are some methods you can totally stop subvocalization:

1. You should point to the words you read when you read

If your reading is done, will hear you speaking the words that you have in your head. This can help you stay in your spot. In order to replace the need to be in a position to stay it is easy to draw the words using your fingers. Your eyes won't wander so easily.

2. A-E-I-OU

It is possible to stop subvocalization by repeating the vowels in all five vowels over and over and. This can get irritating however it can be helpful in the long run , when you're first trying to stop using the words you think of in your head. If you are distracted of a different thought in your head as reading, you won't be able to think of the words printed on the page simultaneously. This can train your brain to recognize what you're seeing instead of having to actually think about it.

3. You can distract yourself

The act of distracting yourself can aid in understanding how it is easy for you to stay busy when you study. If you are able to keep your mind occupied, you are likely to break the routine you've been enslaved to for the majority years. Chewing gum and bouncing your knee counting, or even just talking about anything can distract you and will allow you to browse through the pages.

4. Try to read more quickly than usual, even in the event that you don't be able to register everything

Before you test this method for a article or book first, practice it at home, first with an article, novel perhaps even an essay. It is all you need to do is make yourself read more quickly than you're used to. This could mean that you will be unable to understand everything you read initially, but eventually you'll get habit of it and will get more efficient; sufficient to be able to use it in school or workbooks and assignments.

Another method to improve your reading speed is to be aware of "back skipping" Back skips occur to many people and like subvocalization, they are human natural. If you do back skip you are able to go backwards and trying to focus on the word or phrase you've already read. This can happen without conscious thought but it may also be something occurs by accident when you lose focus or become distracted. To stop this from happening the only thing you need to do is look out for it. There aren't a variety of tricks you can learn to prevent these types of events. My suggestion to you is to be focused on the content you're reading without getting distracted--to not have to do to re-read.

Place a piece of paper under the line is being read or drawing your finger over the text is another method that will help you read more quickly and also improve your focus.

The speed at which you learn languages is faster.

It is a dream we all would like to learn. Yet, there are those who say the process takes years of intensive studying and actual interactions to learn the language. But is that really true? Accelerated learning reveals that there are numerous ways you can work at home in order to master the language and be proficient within about a year.

The first thing you must do is purchase an application for your phone that will help you learn the language. A majority of apps, like Duolingo, Babbel, or Rosetta Stone can help you to learn languages in a fun way and even help you create games from it. We have already learned, from the beginning of chapter one that playing an activity from your study will make it much simpler to learn.

It is also possible to begin with the most popular phrases and words. This can make it simpler to master and remember. It may also assist to apply what you have learned to other words and phrases. For instance for example, for instance, in French when you wish to use the phrase, "I like pizza" the French equivalent would be "J'aime la pizza." You can even conclude that "j'aime" means "I enjoy." This could aid in identifying other words in French.

One-on-1 tutoring and teaching is something you ought to consider. When you have someone else to study with, it can to motivate you to learn. If you're an athlete and you want to make it a an event out of it!

Chapter 12: Discipline, Not Motivation

There is a certain thing that happens to many people each year which I personally find quite bizarre. Certain amounts of time is passed (365 days, to be precise) and suddenly, those who seemed content to let their lives go bynow have a determination to start working on all the things they'd like to do and ought to be doing since the beginning.

"I'm planning to be into good shape!" Bob yells.

"I'm going to be going to that place!" says Katie.

"I'm going to do everything I ought to have done this season!" says the random person to whom no one has invited to the party.

These are just a few of the possible things that people could share with their guests at a typical New Year's Eve celebration. And what are these phrases? Yes, "New Year's Resolutions".

There isn't any inherent problem when making such assertions. There is an energy that is tangible about the approaching new year. it brings the notion of a fresh start by let go of the burdens from the previous year as well, and in some sense changing into a completely new person.

The thing that people who make these claims seem to overlook but although they've got a newfound determination to achieve what they want to achieve, they're the same person they were on January 1st they were on December 31. I'm sure that's the case for me, and likely you're aware, finding the spark that will ignite the process of improving your life can be difficult. It requires a conscious determination to make it happen You could say it's possible that keeping a New Year's resolution could be that ignition, yet I've observed that it's a plan which usually burns out pretty quickly since it is more dependent on motivation more than actual discipline.

What's the difference between them is the question you're asking? For a good instance, consider two automobile owners who purchase their vehicles on the same day. One of them is known as Motivation while another is known as Discipline.

Motivation buys his vehicle fresh. It's brand new out of the garage, comes with the full tank of gas, and the fresh car smell. It's ready for the road. Motivation climbs in the car, and before putting the pedal into the ground and putting the pedal to the floor, he promises self that he'll take good care of the new baby. It appears at first to be going smoothly however, the main issue is that this man is pretty uncaring of his car, despite fact that he promised himself that he would maintain it after the time came to purchase it. He doesn't have the oil changed on a regular basis, and is able to leave the car outside during winter months for several days without even starting an engine in order to heat it. When enough time passes the brand new car begins to fail more frequently, the mechanical parts begin to wear out, and then eventually, the car isn't running at all.

Let's take a look at the other owner who is Discipline. The same day Motivation was taking his vehicle from the dealer, Discipline browses the classifieds of the local paper and comes across an older used model that has a good amount of miles, but is running well. He takes it home and turns out to be the exact opposite car owner than Motivation was. Discipline makes the effort for changing the oil of his vehicle and makes sure to start the vehicle in winter months, and makes sure to keep the car well taken by. A couple of years later (pun not intended) when Motivation's car fails for the final time and is taken away for scrap, Discipline's car has accumulated 160,000 miles, and is running just like the day he bought it.

That's right, there's likely to be the most significant distinction between discipline and motivation The motivation decreases, and discipline holds its own.

Although motivation is helpful in achieving immediate goals, like clearing a room or getting rid of the garbage, it's not able to translate to the long run due to a couple of specific reasons that I'll outline in this article:

1. It's an endurance race and not it's a sprint

The biggest issue that people with motivation have to contend with, that disciplined people typically have is fatigue, which typically occurs when trying to complete something. When motivation is present to someone is arouses them to have a strong desire to begin something that they've put off for some time. They'll go to at the gym or are likely to begin learning the instrument. With the drive that's so strongly connected to motivation make the first step needed to start aiming for that target.

They buy the gym membership or guitar, and may even workout initially, or perhaps devote a few hours each week practicing chords on the guitar. However, since it was drive that drove them to take on these activities initially the fire eventually will fade, in the event that they cannot transform their motivational attitude to an organized one.

It's a sad fact that the majority of highly individuals who are motivated, they wish to get ahead quickly without investing the time and effort to achieve it. They'd like to get in shape in the gym or capable of shredding killer solos on guitar without doing the work that can only be completed by a person who is well-organized. Sure, you can mention a few individuals who, as it appears to have their successes incorporated to their D.N.A. The legendary Jimi Hendrix was a master in the guitar from an young age, and He spent hours practicing his art. Motivation is a problem that it makes people believe that all they require is the desire to achieve success in whatever they're working towards, but in reality the desire must be coupled with a disciplined, disciplined work ethic and a strict schedule that is followed.

2. All it takes is your mind.

Another issue in motivational behavior is the fact that it may be a surprise and deceiving. Referring to the instance of someone who is suddenly motivated to purchase an gym membership or buy a guitar it's the norm that just the action of doing these things can give them feelings of satisfaction.

They may think to themselves, "Wow, I spent real money, so that means I'm really committed to sticking to this!"

However, this is seldom the scenario. The first step to something and not because they have an established plan that they can adhere to, but because they are motivated to take the step, it means they don't see the forests to the woods. Sure, purchasing a gym membership is among the essential things to take care of before he can begin doing solid workouts, However, if one goes there without an established workout routine that he could follow, he's likely going to do some unplanned dumbbell curls or walking a bit on a treadmill and later going home , not being certain of what he should do (if it appears like I'm quoting my own personal experience, it's since I'm). There won't be any good workouts, and that means that he will not begin to see any improvements after which he'll become disillusioned and stop exercising for a period of time with no results.

If the person is exercise is a disciplined one is a disciplined one, he'll develop a well-planned workout program and a routine that he'll stick to. The gym will be a place where he'll go and complete the workout over time. I can guarantee the person who is doing this will begin seeing results, whereas the one who's motivated just remains at home and wonders what's wrong with his love handles that they won't be able to take a dive.

3. There is no better time than now

I'm not trying to judge anyone who's ever made an attempt to keep a New resolution for the New Year. I've done itmyself, my family and friends have made it happen and you are among the readers who are more than likely to have completed it. I hope that at the close of this chapter you'll be able to see the mistake of your actions, just as I have.

The most significant issue in these resolutions - aside from their fact they're driven from motivation and likely not be successful it is that they allow the person to delay improving themselves for a certain period of time. I'm not kidding when I say that I've been in the presence of people who claimed that in September their aim to start the new year was to eat better. What the person really meant was "I'm going allow myself to continue eating a diet that is unhealthy for the next three and a quarter months."

It's a real baffling thought For me personally, since we all are aware that we must take a step back to make us better, and yet we tell ourselves "I'll be able to do it soon or in the future" or "Once the *blank* has changed, I'll begin to"blank". I know I know, it's our nature to find excuses however if you truly desire to become an organized person this is a undesirable habit you must to eliminate.

The thing you have to be able to accept is that there's no reason not to begin doing what you'd like to do right now. There is simply no time like today. The time is short and uncertain By putting off getting better at yourself in the long run, you're actually leaving yourself with less time to make it happen in the event that you decide to begin making yourself better.

Chapter 13: What You Can Do You Can Enhance Your Memory and learn faster

It is essential to learn quickly. aspect if you wish to stand out in your class or receive an increase in your job. But , it's not worth learning when you aren't able to recall the correct information at the time you require it.

Experts in learning like cognitive psychologists and psychologists who study developmental psychology have found various factors which could help you enhance your memory and be more efficient in learning.

Innovative Strategies to Improve Memory Recall

These tips can aid in increasing the chances to retain your memory.

1. Pay attention to the Content you are studying

Attention is a vital aspect of memory. In order to improve recall, information needs to be transferred from short-term memory into long-term memory. Your brain is able to do this by focusing your concentration on the content your studying.

It is best if you have a specific area where you can focus your attention. It could be a spot in your space that is unaffected from distractions like television, street noise or music and other distractions.

Being away from distractions can be challenging, especially when you share a room with a friend or have children who are small. It is possible to schedule your study time , and make certain that your roommate is aware of the specific time and can give you time. You can also request your spouse to look after your children, so that you can concentrate to your study.

2. Avoid Multitasking

Making laundry and doing laundry all at once makes it even more difficult to concentrate on the subject matter needs to be learned. Although it might seem that multitasking can assist you in achieving more but research has proven that performing multiple tasks simultaneously can affect your efficiency and accuracy. If you're looking to gain knowledge, make certain that you're not doing anything else while you're studying.

3. Plan regular study sessions

Maintaining a consistent study plan will stop you from over-studying. This will allow you the time to be able to process the necessary details. Studies have shown that students who study regularly retain the material more efficiently than those who study in the evening prior to the exam.

4. You must organize and structure the information you are learning

Information is organized into similar clusters. This structure can be utilized by organizing the material you're learning. It is ideal to put the same concepts and terms or draw an outline of the readings and notes to aid you to organize your concepts.

5. Utilize mnemonics for better memory recall

Mnemonics are effective strategies that you can employ to assist with better memory. In essence, a mnemonic can be described as a method of retaining information. It is possible to identify a particular set of ideas that you are able to remember by referring to an everyday term you are able to recall easily. The ideal is to have mnemonics employed with humor, fun and captivating images. You can make up an anthem, a rhyme or joke, that can aid in recalling information.

Name mnemonics can be used as well as expression mnemonics. An excellent example of an acronym for name is PVT. TIM HALL for remembering the names of the essential amino acids: Phenylanine,

Valine, Threonine, Tryptophan, Isolucine, Histidine, Arginine, Leucine and Lysine.

Below are some instances of expressions mnemonics.

To quickly recall Henry's Law: Pressure may increase gas's solubility. You can apply this expression to bring back memories of the good old' Henry, take note of the bubbles present in your shaken Cola you had.

For easy recall of Boyle's Law, which states that the pressure of gas is ininversely proportional to volume when at constant temperature, it is possible to use this expression : Boyle's Law is the most effective because it presses gas very tiny.

6. Practice makes perfect

To be able to better recall information, it is necessary to infuse what you're learning in long-term memory. For instance, if you require to master key chemical terms You can research the terms you are studying and then go on to go through a more thorough explanation on the meaning behind that word. After you've practiced this technique repeatedly, you'll be able to see that retrieving information is much simpler.

While doing the actual use of the concept will assist you in recalling. So, simply studying chemical equations isn't enough. It is essential to try out your theories in the lab.

Connect new concepts to the things You're accustomed to

When you're learning about something that is new to you, contemplate about how this concept is connected to things you already know. When you link new ideas to your previous memories it will significantly boost your chances of recalling details that you've recently acquired.

For instance, if you are studying calculus consider ways you could apply the concepts in everyday situations like how you could apply the concepts to everyday routine life, such as electricity, magnetism, and so on.

Visualize Ideas to Increase Recall and Memory

You can improve your memory and recall when you can visualize the information you're studying. Perhaps you've noticed that it is simpler to learn from a book that is filled with graphs, illustrations and illustrations. If you're not able to find a visual clues to aid you then you can.design your own. You can draw figures and charts with your notes, or you can make use of different colours of pens or highlighters to organize related concepts in the study material.

Introduce New Information to your colleague

Research has shown that reading out loud significantly increases memory retention. Researchers have also found that teaching new knowledge to others increases understanding and helps in retrieving information. This strategy can be used to your own study by imparting the information you've learned to a roommate, classmate or study buddy.

Double your efforts to concentrate on the difficult learning material

Did you know that it is much easier to remember information from the chapters that begin and end? The sequence in which the information is presented may play a part in the recall. This is called the serial position effect.

While finding the information within the pages of a book can be a challenge You can solve this issue by investing additional time to work on the concepts. It is also possible to restructure the information you've learned to be simpler to remember. If you encounter an idea that is difficult to grasp it is possible to put in an extra effort to fully grasp and grasp the information.

Change Your Study Habits in a while

Another way to boost memory is to alter your habits of study once in the course of time. If you've been studying in your room for three days then try moving to a different area to begin your next study plan. If you're studying in the night, you can take a few minutes each morning to go over the ideas you've studied. Find a more innovative method of how you learn. By doing this, you will improve the effectiveness of your work and significantly increase your long-term memory.

Get enough rest

Another areathat researchers are currently examining is the impact that sleep deprivation can have on the process of learning. In the absence of enough sleep, we tend to be less attentive, alert and focused, making it more difficult to absorb information. The lack of sleep causes over-worked neurons, which are unable to more effectively link information. We also have less capacity to remember prior information.

Additionally our interpretation processing can be affected. The ability to make sound choices is affected since our brain isn't capable of assessing the situation and respond to it. Our judgment is impaired.

The effects of fatigue can affect our capacity to learn. Organ systems don't function optimally and muscles aren't relaxed and neurons aren't firing quickly. Inattention lapses caused by sleeping disorders can lead in physical injuries and accidents. This is especially important for those who are doing hands-on training such as machines and sports.

Sleep deprivation can have negative affects on the mood of an individual and affects the ability to learn. Changes in mood affect our ability to learn new information and, consequently, retain that information. Even though chronic sleep deprivation affects individuals differently (and the consequences aren't fully understood) It is an established fact that quality sleep can have an effect that is positive on memory and learning.

The NASA Nap

Napping seems to be a common practice for lazy people, but studies suggest that it could assist you in increasing your ability to learn, regardless of whether you're a pro at rocket propulsion, or are have just started learning knit.

Since 1995 NASA carried out a specific study among their pilots in order to assist them improve their alertness and focused, which is essential for their work. The results of the study indicates that a 26-

minute rest in the air (while NASA pilots are still at work) NASA pilots remain working) enhanced their efficiency by 34% and overall alertness by 54 percent.

A NASA nap will help you gain knowledge and is an effective way to unwind your mind and body. The best time to take the NASA nap is from 1pm and 4 pm. You must also lie on your back with your head and your upper body elevated (like sitting) to prevent REM as well as deep sleep.

In the case of a huge task, it is advised to take a break at lunchtime for a sleep or an esoteric nap. Set your clock timer for 26 minutes. If you'd like to take an extended nap you can set it to 90 minutes so that you'll be able to complete your entire period of sleep and awake refreshed and ready to start learning again.

Exercises

Learn about the strategies that are discussed throughout this article. Select the best strategies you can apply according to the type of material you have to learn. Make sure you practice these techniques frequently.

Chapter 14: The Management of Your Progress

School isn't an easy to master, but one fact that appears to be the case most of the time is that learning outside of school may be a greater challenge. The reason is that learning outside of school typically lacks the disciplined structure of school setting. When you attempt to learn the subject on your own you aren't guided by a qualified instructor who will ensure that you are on the right course in all instances. One of the toughest problems to overcome when you are learning outside of school is the absence of a formal system for grading. It is rare that you get the chance to assess your understanding of the subject the same way you do at school, like with essays or research papers, or even final examinations. The lack of structure could cause it to be difficult to keep track of the progress you are taking in learning about an unfamiliar subject. This is why many to be discouraged and give up before they've completed their learning. If you are unable to track the progress you've made, it can be difficult to believe that you're not making any advancement in any way. Although school grades may be a source of stress , they were also an opportunity for motivation and pride, particularly when you got the perfect grade from your teacher who was known as being difficult to please. Thus managing your progress is as vital as any other way of studying or learning that is described within this guide. The main reason behind monitoring your progress is to alleviate the feeling of not making progress. More complex topics, such as languages are often overwhelming because in theory , they could be an inexhaustible source of learning. It's impossible to master a language entirely. There will always be words that you do not know, or an strange rule that you see in a particular place which you don't know. Furthermore, for every language, there will be several dialects, meaning that nobody can ever master an entire language from beginning to conclusion. This means that it could seem like you're not making any progress, especially even if you don't have standard tests to monitor your learning successes. That's why it's essential to develop the method of keeping the track of your performance. In keeping track of such things as the time you've spent studying a subject and scores from tests on your understanding in the topic, you'll be able to feel an immediate sense of achievement for the effort and time you've put in.

Another reason to track the progress of your child is that it allows you to determine which areas are easy and which areas can be difficult for you during the process of learning about a subject. Mathematics is an excellent illustration of this. A lot of people are wizards in basic mathematics, but struggle with more complicated systems like geometry or algebra. On the other hand, there are people who excel in geometry, but struggle with algebra or a similar scenario. Even though bad grades may seem as a petty punishment, they should ultimately serve as an indication that you have to devote a bit extra time, effort and energy in the subject you are struggling with. Thus, tracking your progress isn't simply about lifting your spirits. It's an issue of controlling your learning process in general.

The most efficient way to keep track of your progress is to regularly take tests. Although tests might not be included with the subject that you are studying, the fact is that tests on every subject are available on the internet with no difficulties. There are many websites accessible that assess your knowledge of the subject at no cost. Making the effort to research these websites along with the assessments they have available can go a long way in helping you get the most out of your studies. If you consistently score high scores on the tests you take, then you must think about boosting your study routine. If, on the other hand, your scores are low or even worse, you need to look at reducing your frequency of study or altering the way you study. In the final analysis, these tests don't have to be meant to prove how competent you are. These tests as well as the scores they offer serve as a way to control the learning process. You must ensure that you are challenging yourself but at the same time, you need to ensure that you're actually understanding the material.

Another advantage of testing is the fact that you are able to take back the exact test at an earlier time. The comparison of scores of the previous exam you attempted with the most recent results can help you get an understanding of your progress achieved. Most of the time, we don't spend the time to go back and check ourselves against older material which is why we don't recognize the amount of progress we have made in a specific topic. In addition, as improving is the most important aspect of understanding any subject and only when we determine how much we've gained can we be sure of what we've learned. In addition to creating a sense that we are progressing, this can also provide an important boost to morale. The prospect of seeing real improvement in your time will be enough to keep any person interested, no matter how difficult or exhausting the process of learning turns out to be.

Chapter 15: Steps To Start Speed Reading

The benefits of Reading

Reading is more than entertain your brain. The research conducted done by Thomas Corley, shows that the majority of self-made millionaires have read at least two books per month? Be aware that they don't read to entertain themselves or pleasure, but to gain knowledge and for education. People who are successful always take into consideration new ideas and that's the reason they became extremely successful and prosperous in the first place.

* Think of Benjamin Franklin, as far in the late 18th century. As scientist, he developed several life-changing inventions including bifocals, a light rod. Not just was he one of the founders who drafted of the Declaration of Independence for the US however, the man also went on succeed as the postmaster general's first. He was certainly a prolific writer and reader.

The famous and wealthy reading habits don't stop there:

* Bill Gates reads around 50 books over the course of a single year. The reason he loves nonfiction is that it allows him to constantly discover new things from the globe. He loves to write notes when he encounters something that is new. He advises you to think of reading as a process of intellectual development to improve your brain's capacity. In the present, he block his time at least for an hour every day to have an intense reading session and not newspapers , but books. Books that enable your brain to constantly learn new knowledge throughout your day.

* Mark Zuckerberg enjoys at least one book every month.

* Elon Musk read two books every day while he grew older.

If you haven't yet done it, you should start reading every day.

Begin today and keep up this routine.

Reading isn't necessary to entertain yourself, but it can provide a good amount of enjoyment. There are other advantages from reading which are crucial. When you diversify your reading materials is the ability to learn. It is not always possible to be accurate, especially when you are focusing on the media. To ensure you have an objective perspective of the world, you must diversify the kind of information you're planning to learn.

Begin by taking a couple of pages from an e-book before going to bed. It is possible to have several novels in your reading pile, switching the genre according to your mood. Find a nonfiction area in life that has always fascinated you, but haven't thought of exploring it. It could be nature, science gardening, the universe. Pick a book about that area and then read it regularly.

Your vocabulary will expand and your memory will improve as you develop your writing skills. Now you have the possibility of a new form of entertainment into your life. You are now part of many people that love reading, which includes those who are self-made millionaires.

Once you're an avid reader, you need to go up a level and master the art of speed read. This is a way of learning even large bits of knowledge and accomplishing it at a fast rate.

The benefits of speed Reading

Imagine the possibilities of processing information faster. Maybe you're a student needing to pack a lot of information in your head to pass your exams or someone who has to sort through piles of papers in their job. Speed reading allows readers to tackle their work much faster and more efficiently.

There's no shame for being a slow reader. Anyone who reads frequently should be proud of this fact. Readers who are slower will not absorb information as quickly as speed readers. It is all it takes to master the techniques for speed reading. This skill will allow you to see the ease of which you can improve your understanding quickly. It's not because you have more time but rather that you improve your brain's ability to be able to process information faster.

It's not the quantity of words your eyes pay attention to when you read however, it's how well the word you are able to identify. When you begin to practice speed reading, you'll begin to miss words that aren't essential. The key to speed reading success is understanding which words you should leave out on and which words you should focus on. However you must be able to comprehend what the meaning of the words you're reading. If you're not learning, you've wasted your knowledge.

You're on the verge of becoming an expert reader by gaining more knowledge about writing. There won't be examinations to prove your new abilities. Because of the extensive exposure to written word your brain will begin to notice the new structure of linguistics on the pages, to the point where it can predict what's coming up before you ever get there.

Learning new skills can be done by exposing your mind to new things that you do not are aware of. This is precisely what you'll be doing when you begin to read different types of texts. For instance, the sentences of a novel may not structured the same way as the words in the scientific paper. The more you are aware of language, the quicker you'll be able to traverse the various writing styles.

How to Read the First Steps of Speed Reading

One of the most basic and most crucial abilities you require to are able to read at a high speed can be "focus." Your brain absorbs the information in such a speed that if you let your mind wander while you read at a fast pace all the words that you read will be lost to memory. "Focus" is the new buzzword since without it, you won't be able to master the art of reading with power.

For the majority of us, as we began learning to read in the early years and read each word on the page. We were taught to run our fingers across the lines of text, reading each word at a snail's-pace. As adults, you no have to read with such a slow rate. When you speed read you speed through books that contain a lot of information. It's all about cutting chunks of text. If you're using a mobile phone, you probably send texts with several abbreviated words inside sentences. You already have the ability to communicate without using every single word in a sentence.

It is essential to use grammar in writing, but when you read you can jump around, skip, and jump across paragraphs, sentences, and even pages.

It is the process of learning to distinguish certain words within a sentence and leaving out the rest. In the sentence above, we have 11 words total. To understand the meaning of this sentence you will only have to read five words.

Here's the complete sentence:

Sentence Example: Once there was an old man wearing large hats.

If you are speed reading, you must to understand the significance of a sentence without needing to read every word. In the below sentence in which you can only read the words in capital letters, are you able to be able to comprehend the meaning of the sentence?

* Example of Sentence A time, there was an MAN who wore a hat.

Two words do not suffice to fully comprehend the meaning behind this sentence. We've taken out the commonly used nouns which form the basis in the phrase. You only know it's about the words "man" and"hat. "hat." It's possible to not be able to interpret the sentence correctly like:

* Translated sentences: "A young man lost his hat" or "a huge man was sitting on his head with his."

By reading only a few words it is difficult to comprehend the meaning that the sentences are describing. Continue adding words until we determine how many words we'll need to be able to comprehend the sentence. What are the ways that our two keywords connect better? We now need to find the descriptive words that are referred to as adjectives.

In this sentence this sentence, we will see these words "old" as well as "big." That means that we have to consider four words:

* Example Sentence There was once an old man wearing an enormous hat.

We aren't quite sure of what the meaning of the sentence is however, we're getting close. We need to find a connecting word, and that is the verb or the word that does. In this case it's the word "wore."

Does the sentence we are discussing be understood by five words?

* Example of Sentence There was a time when there was an old man who wore an enormous hat.

In reading just "Old man wore a big hat" we are able to comprehend the meaning of this sentence. We missed six words while reading this sentence. It's not about the speed of reading but knowing which words to avoid.

There is no need to be aware of what a word, noun, adjective , or verb is, it's likely the brain in a state of being wired to identify the relevant keywords. I just utilized this term in order to explain how you can reduce an 11-word sentence to a five-word sentence.

At this point this kind of reading is still very similar to the method known as skim reading. You must develop other techniques to enhance your ability to speed read.

Chapter 16: Brain Diet

Here are some foods you must and shouldn't take in order to ensure your brain is active, healthy and healthy.
Foods to eat for an Optimal Brain
To boost the condition of your brain, take the following nutrients:
Oily Fish
Oily fish such as tuna, mackerel and herring as well as salmon are fantastic food sources for omega-3 acids which provide nourishment to your whole body, and especially the brain cells, which helps improve their health and function.

To provide your brain with a an adequate amount of omega-3 fats that it requires to be healthy and flourish take at least 100g of oily fish three to six times per week. In addition, you should eat seeds and nuts because they are also rich in omega-3 fats.
Berries
The flavonoid content of berries is high. antioxidants that help flush out toxic substances from your body and help

regulate stress. This helps reduce inflammation in your brain , keeping it healthy. Dark chocolate is another great food source for these vitamins. consume regular portions of dark chocolate and berries.

Whole Grains

High in vitamin E whole grains like brown rice, barley and oatmeal can provide your brain and body the capability to fight off diseases to function at their best and keep you healthy. Be sure to consume at least a cup of whole grain each day to enhance your brain's performance.

Eggs

With proteins, vitamins Bs, along with healthy fats and vitamins, eggs can provide your body with energy as well as nutrients that you require for keeping your mind healthy and healthy. Consume at minimum one egg per day, cooked or poached in case you do not want to cook it with oil or are trying to control your weight.

In addition to the food items mentioned above, you can add avocados, broccoli and kale Brussels sprouts, cauliflower and seeds to your diet to ensure your brain is healthy and strong.

Brain Damaging Foods to Avoid

If you are increasing the amount of these food items, be sure to stay away from food items that contain the following ingredients:

Processed sugar

Sugary foods that contain a lot of processed sugars like sweetened drinks and packaged desserts increase the risk of having high blood pressure, diabetes and heart conditions These are all likely to impact your cognitive and overall health.

Carbohydrates refined

White pasta, bread and white rice carry the highest glycemic load which refers to the amount of blood sugar that is raised by certain foods within your body. When you consume these types of foods, you raise your blood sugar and insulin levels, which could affect the brain's function.

Foods that are high in trans-fats

Trans-fats can be linked to poor memory and cognitive decline, as well as a lower the volume of brain cells, as well as a higher chance of developing Alzheimer's disease. Ready-made cakes, cookies that are packaged in a box frosting, margarine and shortening are all rich in trans-fats. It's best to stay clear of eating these foods frequently.

Be aware of your diet and lifestyle choices. Consider how an item's likely to impact your mind and body before eating it. This will help you make better choices that ensure that your mind, body and heart in good health.

If you apply these diet suggestions and pair them with the other suggestions we have discussed in this article Your brain will flourish and perform at the best levels that is possible.

Chapter 17: The clothing

You might have the ideal outfit for your interview and you feel like you're well-prepared for what's to come. You are confident and content with your appearance and are prepared to conquer the world. When the day for your appointment comes around and you get prepared only to find that your dress isn't quite the way you remembered of a few days earlier.

It's not a rare situation. Even if we don't think we look attractive in the dress does not necessarily mean that something has changed in our physical appearance but working under stress can cause us to be less confident and put our inner struggles to trivial issues like this. Being confident that you'll look great for the job will determine your confidence level that you show. If you go into your interview and feel like you're ugly, then your confidence will drop and you will not be able to conduct the interview in the way you could have.

It's good to have a few different outfits that you can try on the day of your interview. If something doesn't feel right to you , there are alternative alternatives. It's recommended to carry some change of clothes as well as another option for an interview. In the event of an accident, like spilling coffee you can choose a different outfit to change clothes. Change of clothes to something more casual should be taken with you to enable you to remove your dress for the interview, leaving the nice clothes for the next interview. This will give you the chance to relax immediately. You'll be happier in knowing that you don't need to dress in a way that doesn't make you feel the best.

If you are choosing an outfit for an interview it's best to choose pieces that aren't too extravagant. Use solid colors or simple flowing patterns like thin stripes, but definitely no large and bold designs or prints that are out of the ordinary. These types of colors and patterns can be distracting for the interviewer. Just like a blue-mouthed mouth after a snort, they will make your interviewer concentrate more on your attire than your answers. You're hoping to draw their attention, but do not distract them away from your primary mission that is getting to know you.

Your closet should include some basic clothing choices including a white button-down collared shirt, dark skirt, or black pants and an elegant pair of black formal shoes. If you're a woman and decide to put on heels must not wear anything higher than 2 inches. The most appropriate height is the kitten heel, which is not higher than an inch. The reason is because heels affect the way you walk , and you don't need your exit and entrance to be a battle with your heels that are a tad high. Keep your fancy three-inch heels for evening out in town or a cat stroll. Men must also wear a stylish tie that matches their shirt and belt to match their outfit. These are items that will get you far, and although they might not look attractive, they are things that are timeless pieces that are never out of fashion.

Be aware that your interviewer doesn't care the brand you wear. If you're concerned that you're not in tune with the latest trends in fashions, then the main factor is to ensure that the clothing is appropriate for your body. Your clothes should have no holes and must be neatly pressed. Make sure you take care of your clothes prior to your interview and make a plan. Don't throw your dress into the dryer overnight in hopes that it will be dry the next day. There's a chance of having a wet , unpressed clothing.

Make a plan in advance of the various options for clothing and ask a trusted friend for their opinions. Don't wear too exposed clothing, and keep your accessories to the minimal. Some jewelry is acceptable, but stepping into the office of your potential boss in the shape of an alcoholic disco ball is an alarm. There is no reason to employ one who is an ongoing distraction in the workplace.

Remember that we talked about the impact of shoes on your walking. One of the biggest mistakes individuals make is buying new shoes just one or two days prior to their interview. The shoes take time to adjust and the latest pair of shoes could leave you dragging from the office. In the event that you know you'll soon being a candidate for a job buy your new shoes and walk around your house, breaking them into. They will still look good but won't cause blisters or harm to your feet.

Although shoes might not appear to be a significant thing, this is a garment that might require a bit of investment. If you can afford a pair of comfortable and well-constructed formal shoes is usually superior to purchasing a cheap pair to last. In the long run , you could invest more time and money buying cheap pairs of shoes rather than purchasing a pair that will last for years. Most of the time, a well-made pair will also wear better and leave your feet happy.

If you are forced to and must put on new shoes, do yourself a favor by taking the necessary precautions to take to ensure you don't be left with a painful foot. Mole skin, an adhesive-backed anti-rub pad, that can be cut into customized shapes using a pair scissors at home. This tiny piece of fabric with a sticky backing will prevent your shoe from hitting you in the wrong areas and is easily concealed in a sock or beneath a nylon.

Make sure to put the shoes in place. This is an obvious thing to do, but you'll be amazed at the number of people who take their shoes off during an interview. This can cause distraction and look extremely informal. People may view feet as an intimate area of the body or think they are dirty. Don't forget to put on your shoes, even whether they cause discomfort. This is why the right pair an excellent idea.

Hydrogen

These suggestions may seem like a bit self-explanatory, but they're important. Maintaining a clean and healthy daily routine will make these routines simple and effortless those times when you need to attend an important interview or meeting. Your coworkers will be grateful for your cleanliness. Nobody wants to be with one who has an unpleasant smell or who isn't caring for their body.

There are certain conditions that cannot be controlled by the individual and it is important to be compassionate and considerate of the people who are around us. However, should you be able to take care of your body it is essential to practice it. Self-care is a sign of self-worth and shows your prospective employers and coworkers know believe that you are self-confident.

Be sure to brush your hair, and have haircut if needed. If you have hair that is long, ensure that you remove your hair from your face to ensure that you can maintain good eye contact with your interviewer and they will be able to see all parts of you. This will make interacting more easy and they'll have no distractions from the hair that covers your eyes or other parts that cover your face. If you're always putting your fingers through your hair, it is not just a distraction, but it can cause you to appear as if you're insecure.

The process of washing your hair is essential because it is a sign that you've got good self-care routines. In the event that your hair becomes oily or dirty, it could cause a distraction for those who are around you. It's the same for hair on your body. If you're a woman with facial hair, you need to take care to keep it neat and cut.

It is important to inquire with the company you are interviewing regarding hair colors, and. Should they follow a specific rule concerning colors that are not normally present, you'll have to get rid of your favorite hair shades prior to your interview. The reason you'll need to make this change prior to your interview is due to the fact that there are managers who require an applicant who is prepared to take on the job at in the moment, even if they may not start immediately or even immediately. Having your hair dyed could hinder you from running. It's a strange circumstance considering that a boxed hair dye will solve the problem, but in the current market, with the number of applicants who are waiting to be hired, there is a good chance you'll be overlooked when you don't meet the requirements at the time of the first meeting.

As we continue with the topic of hair, make sure you remove hair from areas that could be noticeable. It's a good idea to keep body hair at an absolute minimum, as it may cause body or. Deodorants are an essential requirement. Find a formula that works for you. Also, be aware that you might need to switch formulas in the future when your body gets used to the one you've used for a while. Cleaning your deodorant at night prior to getting to bed will ensure that you are using the full power of the formula you're currently using.

Don't wear perfumed deodorants that are strong in scent such as body sprays, perfumes or fragrances. While they might smell nice to you, there are people at work who might have an allergic reaction to what you're wearing, or feel that they give them headaches or cause distraction. The most effective rule of thumb is to wear only soap. Anything else could cause problems for certain.

Make sure you clean your teeth thoroughly and floss. A clean mouth with fresh breath can make sure that the smell of your mouth isn't a distracting factor. If you work closely with other people at work, they won't be thrilled having to face any discomfort. This can derail meetings that you might have together , and could cause your coworkers to be reluctant to work close to you.

Additionally, although less likely in the event that you do not maintain a healthy oral hygiene, it could affect other areas in your body. Have you ever heard that a person who doesn't practice proper oral hygiene practices is more likely develop heart disease? This is a fact! Dental insurance is a benefit that many businesses offer which you pay for in the present and if you're not taking care of your dental health, you'll pay more, and take more time off from work to take care of something that could have been taken care of with a regular routine.

Awakening

The entire interview process could affect your physical and mental condition. Every person is unique, so the stress may manifest differently. You might need to manage anxiety during the process of interviewing in as well as out of your interview. It is possible that you are in a state of sleeplessness due to anxiety or are completely different and aren't getting enough sleep.

If you're the kind that loses sleep because of nerves, take advantage of your extra energy and make yourself exhausted by taking an easy walk or sitting in meditation. You can drink a tea containing chamomile or take a melatonin supplement if you're sure you're comfortable with it. If you're able drink milk, sipping warm glasses before getting ready for bed can provide similar effects to Melatonin. If you've never tried the melatonin supplement before, even though it is a natural substance this isn't the time to try adding something new to the mix. Try the relaxing.

Don't relax by watching TV or looking at your smartphone or computer screen. Research has shown that looking at moving images or screens when your body is asleep can affect your brain's functioning and keep you from achieving the necessary REM rest cycle. As an adult , you only require 2 hours of sleep deep and up or eight hours rest.

But, if you don't have a method to track your sleeping patterns, it could be difficult to tell when you've reached your required amount of restorative levels. This is why it's crucial to keep your screens away from the bedroom and switch them off about around an hour prior to bedtime in order to give your brain enough time to wind to a halt and begin closing down for the night.

If you feel that your body reacts to stress and becoming nervous, start your day and hit the gym or engage in some exercises at home. Moving your body can hold additional energy in certain the body's parts and we must move to eliminate those jitters. The elimination of any excess energy prior to the interview makes sure that the anxiety doesn't appear suddenly during your interview.

The same is true in the event that we are feeling tired. If you sprint in place or perform some jumping jacks or a few, you will get yourself a boost of energy to help finish the interview. Breathe deeply and inhale good quantities of oxygen since it will help you remain awake. Sometimes , we start feeling tired due to our bodies slowing down, resulting in getting less oxygen. If you take deep, long breaths, oxygen will get into your bloodstream, then to your brain, and then begin the process of getting you up.

If you're still experiencing problems and you feel like you're not able to get up, try taking a vitamin B12. B12 functions in the same way like caffeine, however it does not result in a major slump later on in the day. It is recommended to take vitamin intake on a regular routine is a good idea for keeping your body and mind sharp and healthy. Certain companies have benefits in their benefits plans that reward employees who are physically fit therefore it's not only an incentive to be healthy, but also to ensure your longevity as well as your overall performance at work.

Chapter 18: Enhancing Your Memory

As you improve your ability to pick up new information , you may begin to think what exactly you're going to manage all the information in your brain. It is crucial to master the latest organizational techniques and some methods of making certain that you're memory is able to be able to keep pace with all the things you're striving to accomplish.

What good can a new piece of information do when you aren't able to retain it for long enough to be useful to you? Let's explore some of the most effective methods to help you keep more of it in mind and have a significant impact in how you handle everyday challenges.

Use Associations

To make information stay in your memory it is important to ensure that you have connections that you can make to. Use words to help you understand the information better and also to make it easier to remember. If you are able to connect with the information in a an unusual or unrelated relationship in your mind that way, you're more likely to stick to it easily.

Chunk Things Together

It is essential to organize your thoughts in the process of retaining new information. Consider dividing the information you're examining into smaller chunks so that it is simpler for you to keep. For instance, break a lengthy number into groups of 5 or 4 instead of. The same way we use numbers for phones as well as social security numbers, so you're used to this routine. Do not try to overload yourself with details. Begin by learning small pieces before moving onto the next. connecting them can be more efficient!

Try Rhyming

There's a reason children's books and songs are organized into rhymed forms which makes them simpler to recall and then repeat. It is possible to use this technique even as an adult and it can help in aiding in the retention of many different facts. Think of the rhyme you may have heard about what number of days there are within the month. "30 days includes September the month of September, April, June, and the month of November." Since that rhymes it effortlessly disappears from the tongue, and also helps to keep the facts in your head to use later on. This makes it simpler to remember when you're required to bring it up once more.

Acronyms Can Help

Certain lists or kinds of materials, it is impossible to use rhymes and break them up further. With these kinds of materials, it's possible to come up with a method to transform them into an acronym to aid in better retention. An example that can be used is popular one that is used by schoolchildren. Imagine all the colours of the rainbow and a simpler method of remembering them in the right order is to consider the word ROY G. BIV. Yellow, red, orange blue, green violet and indigo are names that are difficult to remember than the simple and short acronym.

Try using an Acrostic

Another trick for memory that may be useful for you to master is to create an acrostic using the information you want to recall. This is similar to making an acronym, however instead of making a brand new word, you construct an acrostic using the initial letters of the word. Consider, for instance, the compass's directions, North, East, South and West. It is easier to remember these by a chant such as, "Never eat soggy worms." The most important thing is to make them distinctive or out of kilter slightly so that they make an impression on you.

Conclusion

This book has explained and examined Accelerated Learning. It's not just about the quick consumption of information. It is a more comprehensive method that fulfills the classic educational goals: changing to improve the quality of life of the truth, as well as the change of the student into an intelligent and critical thinker. Students are immersed in the subject for a brief duration of time, and are able to engage in intensive sessions through discussions and exercises.

Rote learning can have merits. Learning to remember numbers and words should be practiced at times.

However, long-term retention information requires motivation and significance. For the best results an effective education program examines the meaning of the subject and draws the curiosity and interest of the students. It's fun. The critical thinking techniques and systems are designed to prompt questions and thoughts, while also enhancing the students' awareness and concern.

Critical thinking is founded on an outline of scientific method reasoning, reasoning, and argument. The observant is more likely to distinguish impressive or rhetorical phrases using well-founded reasoning. They must be able to recognize the biases that affect claims, including political, social standing or personality, and other factors. Writers and speakers must be able justify their claims using the evidence of logic and proof. There's a proven method to accomplish this. The top AL programs will anticipate this and devise strategies to help students to improve their critical thinking abilities.

Learning is best recognized as a social event. Classrooms even in the online classroom is made up of a group of students with shared desires and interests who participate the same learning process. The interaction with teachers and classmates helps students understand the concepts and terms being taught. It incites questioning. An effective AL program provides lots of interaction with the classroom in various ways to encourage deep understanding and appreciation for the subject. The curriculum must be well organized.

The most effective AL program gives students ample opportunities to read and also teaches students to read the content of the subject. It is essential to draw attention to the thesis statement and other important points. It is a skill that requires the ability to sum up effectively. Students may seek out assistance and training in speed taking notes and reading. Students and teachers must be organized and well-organized to efficiently execute and take part in the teaching course. They must organize the teaching and learning. There are a variety of tools and sources. Documents should be stored in well-labeled and well-labeled files, in one place, possibly electronically and backed up with printed forms. Instructors can use computer programs to organize their classes, and organize and categorize material and information for their students and themselves. Students can get the summaries and views of the most important authors, theories, as well as texts, and can download software to take notes. Teachers can provide additional materials including videos and other questions.

There are certifications and training courses to AL teachers and learners. Additionally, local institutions offer some classes with AL form.

AL is an effective and efficient method to teach and learn that will bring the delight of students and instructors. In these frantic and challenging times, where people are constantly moving and adapting to changing technology, places job opportunities, and other knowledge, AL is a wise option that will ease the adjustments and make education and training easier to access. Try it the next time you have to master or instruct something.

www.ingramcontent.com/pod-product-compliance
Lightning Source LLC
Chambersburg PA
CBHW060334030426
42336CB00011B/1339